Boston Bound

A 7-Year Journey to Overcome Mental Barriers
and Qualify for the Boston Marathon

ELIZABETH CLOR

To my loving husband, Gregory Clor, who lifted me up when I had fallen.

ACKNOWLEDGEMENTS

Special thanks to Coach Andrew Lemoncello and The McMillan Running Company for helping me run faster than I ever dreamed possible. I'd also like to thank the RWOL women for their support over these past eight years. Special thanks as well to the ThinkFast women, who originally encouraged me to run marathons and who supported me during my early years of running. My gratitude also extends to Dr. Neal Bowes, without whom this book would not be possible. Finally, I would like to thank my mother and my husband; my mother for editing the book three times, and my husband for giving me the idea to write it, believing in me and supporting me every step of the way.

CONTENTS

FOREWORD

Running a marathon is undoubtedly a physical challenge. What is often overlooked is the mental challenge of not only running the race, but also just getting to the start line. *Boston Bound* is an insight into a seven-year personal journey of uncovering and addressing the mental challenges that accompany marathon running. This inspiring story journals the emotional ups and downs, successes and failures, tears and cheers, and ultimate reward of reaching a dream goal of running the Boston Marathon.

Like many marathon runners, Elizabeth Clor started her journey as a recreational runner. After some initial successes she hit a number of mental roadblocks. As her anxiety grew and her confidence shrunk, her performances suffered—culminating with her being unable to finish several marathons. *Boston Bound* charts her journey through these difficult times as she struggled with her internal thoughts and feelings while seeing many of her teammates and friends enjoy success.

Personal insight into the mental challenges of perfectionism, anxiety, lack of self-confidence, and emotional struggles will touch the reader. Elizabeth felt stuck and out of control as she seemed to be spiraling away from her dreams. She eventually made the often difficult decision to accept that she needed help in pursuing her goals and overcoming her internal struggles.

Boston Bound details Elizabeth's experiences and skills

learned in seeking out my support as a performance expert. Like many runners, Elizabeth's primary focus, and judgements of success, were on her race times, as opposed to the process of achieving them. Further, her identity was closely intertwined with her running accomplishments, which had left her vulnerable to emotional ups and downs. Through a progressive program, we worked through her core beliefs and negative emotions to rewire her brain for success, freeing her from the misconceptions she held about herself and her sport.

Through personal reflection, she started to overcome self-limiting thoughts, deal with her maladaptive perfectionism, and challenge her negative thought processes. As she progressed, she learned and applied critical mental skills such as having a process focus, building robust confidence, planning and strategizing for races, and ultimately believing in her mental capacity to cope and excel in race conditions.

During this transformation, readers live through the lens of Elizabeth as she turns the corner, takes important steps in her development and ultimately claims her place in the 2016 Boston Marathon. This story gives all readers inspiration and hope in overcoming their mental struggles in pursuit of their dream goals.

Boston Bound is a must-read not only for marathon runners in pursuit of their own personal goals, but also for everyone in their journey through life and the internal obstacles we all encounter. I hope you will be inspired.

Neal Bowes, Ph.D.

PART I

A DREAM

CHAPTER 1:
A DREAM IN MOTION

October 2, 2011

I lay flat on my back in the yard of a stranger's house several miles outside of Milwaukee, Wisconsin. Hundreds of marathon runners pass by, and I watch in agony because I can remember how exhilarating it feels to be at mile 20 of a marathon, heading strongly and confidently toward the finish line. It's been over three years since I've experienced that high, despite spending every day of my life dedicated to attaining it again.

My husband, Greg, stands over me with his arms extended, urging me to get up from the ground. I refuse. I tell him to continue on without me—I don't want to ruin his race. Why should my own misery impact his experience? He reminds me that I'm not injured and perfectly capable of getting up from the grass and continuing on with the race. Even so, I resist. I simply don't have it in me to keep going. What would the point be? I've been training my ass off for over three years, and yet I keep failing miserably at the marathon.

It should have been so simple and straightforward to qualify for the Boston Marathon. I put in the hard work and training, I'm fitter and faster than I've ever been in my entire life, and yet I can't bring myself to take one more step forward. It's so embarrassing. Humiliating, even—that I can be so confident in my athletic abilities but in over three years' time, never deliver.

I wish that this was a dream, and that I would soon wake up in my Milwaukee hotel room to find that the race was still hours from starting. After all, I've had numerous nightmares about marathon disasters, so this experience would fit perfectly into my dream life. But unfortunately, I am not lying on a bed. Underneath my back is the very real, hard ground.

In complete emotional anguish, I remain firmly planted on the grass, paralyzed.

* * *

August 30, 2015

In three weeks and one day, I'll be able to do something that I've wanted to do for the past eight years of my life: register for the Boston Marathon. "Wanted" isn't a strong enough word. Strived for? Nope, not strong enough. Longed for? Nah—too saccharine. Dreamed about? Well, at least that's how it all started.

In 2007, I wrote a post in my Myspace blog in which I discussed the differences among plans, goals, dreams, and fantasies. Qualifying for the Boston Marathon fell into the "dreams" category at that point. My marathon times were nowhere near fast enough for Boston to seem feasible, but I thought that if I continued to progress, I might get there eventually.

Participating in the Boston Marathon is considered to be the epitome of a successful running career by many. Because only the fastest marathon runners can secure an entry into this race, it's extremely prestigious within the running community and a goal for many recreational runners with a competitive spirit.

That's how I initially approached qualifying for the Boston Marathon—as someone who enjoyed the personal satisfaction of running marathons and wanted to get to the next level. But at some point, things progressed far beyond having a "competitive spirit." What began as a far-away dream gradually transformed into a vicious cycle of self-inflicted torture. Depression, sleeplessness, starvation, anxiety, isolation, and a slew of other "symptoms" characterized my pursuit of this one prestigious race.

It took me seven years to qualify for the Boston Marathon.

Ironically, if I hadn't tied myself up in knots trying to prove that I was worthy of the Boston Marathon, I probably would have already run the race several times. And I wouldn't be writing this story. But now I have a story to tell, and it's about much more than a sporting event. It's about chasing after a dream, and how it can define you, destroy you, and rebuild you.

Sound dramatic? Well, it was. I had a love/hate relationship with the Boston Marathon, with running, and with myself. The word "neutral" wasn't part of my vocabulary, but over time I've learned that neutrality is the key to success in the sport. Ultimately, if it weren't for my relentless attempts at qualifying for the Boston Marathon, I wouldn't be the person I am today. Just like running a marathon, the only way out of it was through it.

* * *

I was on TV. I never saw the broadcast, but a reporter from the local Virginia Beach news station interviewed me as I stood at the start line of the Shamrock Marathon on March 17, 2008. The reporter approached me, seemingly randomly, and asked me about my plans for this race.

"This is my sixth marathon in two years and I'm hoping to beat my best time by a few minutes," I said with a nervous excitement in my voice. "I'm optimistic about the possibility, but I don't know how much of a factor the wind will be. Even so, I feel ready to run!" The reporter thanked me for my comment and I felt giddy inside.

My marathon history was flawless. Each of my first five marathons had been faster than the previous ones—they were all Personal Records (PRs). Starting in May 2006 with the Delaware Marathon, I was able to shave off at least five minutes each time I ran a marathon:

- May 2006: Delaware in 4:46:28 (10:55 minutes per mile)
- October 2006: Marine Corps in 4:24:39 (10:05 minutes per mile)
- January 2007: Miami in 4:13:54 (9:41 minutes per mile)
- April 2007: New Jersey in 4:05:44 (9:22 minutes per mile)

- November 2007: Richmond in 3:56:41 (9:01 minutes per mile)

Now, I was at the start line of marathon #6, hoping to continue the trend. After speaking with the reporter, I got into race mode. I observed the weather—low 40's, overcast, and very light rain. I was a bit chilly in my running skirt and a lightweight long-sleeved shirt, but I knew I'd warm up after running the first few miles. In fact, these were ideal weather conditions for running.

As I had told the reporter, I felt ready for this. I had put in the training, run a few tune-up races, and developed a race strategy. What's more, I was ready—ready to take whatever the race gave me, ready to deal with the potential wind, and ready to push hard.

The race started, and I knew exactly what to do. With five successful marathons under my belt, I knew to start at a pace that felt easy and to focus on staying relaxed. I had an iPod and a carefully crafted playlist created specifically for the occasion. For me, music was a key part of the marathon experience. Not only did music make the race more enjoyable, but it also motivated me through the tough parts.

As the race progressed, I started to get into a nice rhythm. Once the "easy" early miles were done and the kinks were worked out, I was ready to run a strong race. At the halfway point, I became even more optimistic about having a good race with a PR. I knew how a marathon was supposed to feel at the halfway point. It was supposed to feel like I was working at a medium-hard effort, but nothing was supposed to hurt yet. Everything was supposed to still feel energized and not strained.

I crossed the halfway marker in 1:54:50, which is an average pace of 8:46 for the first half. This was faster than expected, but it felt good so I just went with it. Shortly before mile marker 14, the crowd thickened. I found it hard to maintain my pace because the road had narrowed, with room for just four people across. I realized that there were suddenly more people around me because the 3:50 pace group had caught up with me, and it was a large group. The winds were still heavy, so I drafted off of the group during that portion.

As I approached mile 21, the 3:50 pace group started to get

ahead of me. I could still see the 3:50 flag in the distance, but I was no longer with the pack. I was running alone. I came up with two new mind games on the spot. The first one was to visualize the mile marker pulling me toward it. I thought, "The mile marker wants me! The mile marker needs me! It's tugging at me!" And that really helped as I convinced myself not to stop running in pursuit of mile marker 23, 24, and 25.

It was tough. I had to dig really, really deep to find every ounce of energy and motivation within me. I started telling myself that this pain was temporary. It wouldn't last long. The race glory would last forever, but this pain and this situation were very, very temporary; and if I stopped running, it would only prolong the pain. So I kept repeating to myself over and over again, "Temporary. Temporary. Temporary." And it helped immensely. I persevered. I did slow my pace a little bit, but I didn't walk. Every muscle and every fiber of my being was in so much pain. But I kept repeating "temporary, temporary, temporary," to myself and it gave me the mental strength to push through to the finish.

I passed the mile 26 marker and I only had 0.2 mile left to go! At this point, I surprised myself and put forth an effort that I previously couldn't have imagined. I had run five strong marathons previously, but never had I put forth this kind of effort and demonstrated this much mental willpower. I glanced down at my watch and I realized that I could finish the race in under 3:52. I told myself, *your job is to get to that finish line before your watch reads 3:52. Go for it now!* My eyes were planted firmly on the finish line arch. I focused on my running form. I told myself that I really, really, wanted to break 3:52.

And I did it! I finished the Virginia Beach Shamrock Marathon 2008 in 3:51:49. Another shiny new PR by 4 minutes and 52 seconds. What a high! What an amazing feeling to work so hard and have it pay off with my fastest marathon time yet.

At that moment, running the Boston Marathon was no longer a far-off dream in my mind—it seemed completely attainable. I now only needed to reduce my time by 11 minutes—down to 3:40. Qualifying for Boston felt like the next logical step in my running career. So much so, that I couldn't imagine what it would be like to *not* qualify or worse—not continue my streak of PRs. I expected the marathon joyride to continue all the way to Boston, and I didn't anticipate any bumps in the road. This expectation was my first mistake, and Shamrock would be my last marathon success for years to come.

* * *

I spent quite a bit of time basking in my Shamrock Marathon success. The notion that I was becoming a "fast" runner was exhilarating. I was a perfectionist and nothing satisfied me more than seeing my hard work pay off in such a tangible manner. It wouldn't be long before I was a Boston qualifier.

Four weeks later, I ran the London Marathon as a "fun run," intentionally going at a slower pace than I was capable of so that I could soak in the experience. I set a soft goal of 4:13:08 to mimic the date of the race, but as I approached the finish line, I realized I was a few minutes early and crossed anyway. Once London was complete, it was time to get serious about my plan to qualify for Boston.

I chose the Hartford Marathon in Connecticut as my target race. Like the majority of marathons in the country, the USA Track & Field Association had sanctioned it as an official 26.2-mile course, which was all that was needed for the event to be an official Boston qualifier. It was a quick flight to Hartford from my home in northern Virginia, and I would be able to get a hotel very close to the start/finish area. I thought there would be minimal crowding on the course, but that there would be enough people to generate a nice group of spectators. The weather was supposed to be perfect for running in early October in Hartford, and the race had a great reputation.

As soon as I settled on Hartford, I started putting together my training plan. I knew that in order to shave 11 minutes off of my marathon time, I needed to train harder. I purchased the book *Advanced Marathoning* by Pete Pfitzinger and Scott Douglas, based on the recommendation of some people I respected within the running community. I read the book cover to cover, highlighting the parts that I thought were most important to remember. I was excited and motivated to train "by the book" and transform myself into an "advanced marathoner." The book also included detailed training programs, and I chose an 18-week plan that peaked at 55 miles per week.

For the Shamrock Marathon, I had only been able to train for the eight weeks leading up to the race. I had been injured previously and unable to run for about three weeks at the end of December and first part of January. Once I resumed training, I averaged about 40 miles a week, with a peak of 45. So this new training program would be quite a shift. It would require running as much as 12 miles in the morning before work on a treadmill, but I was prepared for the commitment. I figured that if I could set a 5-minute PR on just 8 weeks of training, I could certainly take another 11 minutes off of my time with 18 weeks of training and higher mileage. I'd qualify for Boston—no problem.

* * *

My Myspace blog had a large following. It received as many as 50 comments per post, mainly from fellow runners. It all started back in 2005 when I used a photo of myself running a half marathon as my profile picture. I received an influx of friend requests from other runners, and I didn't even consider myself a "runner" at that point. I had only run a single half marathon and thought the photo was cool, so I used it as my profile picture.

I blogged about everything: my love life (or lack thereof), my career in marketing, my social life, random thoughts and opinions, and of course, my running. My sole purpose for blogging was to have an outlet for my thoughts and feelings. I also followed quite a few Myspace blogs and developed a close-knit circle of virtual friends whom I had never met in person. This circle of friends was ultimately formalized as the "Big Cat Race Team." We were a group of runners who shared our running experiences on Myspace. The group officially started at some point in 2007 with myself and about 10 other people, and ultimately grew to over 100 people.

In addition to Myspace, I frequented the Runner's World Online forums. When I set out to train for a BQ, I created a discussion thread for women trying to BQ in a fall marathon. Similar to the Big Cat Race Team, this online discussion group started out with just a few women and grew to be quite large over time.

These two online communities played a major role in my running in 2007 and 2008 before I met my husband and stopped spending so much time online. The Big Cat Race Team had runners of all ages and abilities, and I interacted with people from all over the country. We even traveled to races to meet in person, and it added another dimension to running.

The Runner's World Online group was different because we all had so much in common with each other—each of us spending a significant amount of time each week training to get that Boston Marathon qualifying time. We'd post our workouts on a daily basis, and I loved having a dedicated group of women who were interested in my daily training. I also enjoyed following other women's training on a daily basis. The group provided a sense of community so I didn't feel like I was trying to BQ alone.

By the end of the summer of 2008, I'd successfully gotten through a substantial portion of my *Advanced Marathoning* training plan. I followed the plan to the letter, running 50-55 miles per week—and I could tell I was getting fitter and faster. Naturally, with this level of commitment and accomplishment, I felt confident about my ability to qualify for Boston. Particularly when comparing it to my level of training for Shamrock.

On Labor Day weekend, I ran the Virginia Beach Rock 'n' Roll Half Marathon. My plan was to run it as a "tune-up" race to test my fitness level, and then run the Hartford Marathon six weeks later. I was excited about both races, and based on the paces of my training runs, the BQ seemed completely within my grasp. I was shooting for a time of 1:47:00 in the half marathon and was essentially looking for evidence that I was fit enough to qualify for Boston.

Despite all the hard work and effort I had put into training, the half marathon ended up being a complete disaster. I ran a 2:03:36, which was my slowest half marathon in two years. I couldn't handle the heat and humidity and I slowed down to a crawl during the second half of the race. I wasn't even able to come close to my goal in such unfavorable conditions. I was devastated, but at the same time, I knew that my horrendous performance was a direct result of the weather, and not a reflection on my fitness.

The day after the race, I woke up to a killer sore throat, flu-like symptoms and extreme lethargy—I could barely move. I knew I had over exerted myself during the half marathon, but I didn't expect to wake up feeling so miserable. I had noticed a slight sore throat the day before the race, so I figured I must have been coming down with this illness before the half marathon, and I didn't do my immune system any favors by running it. Because simply walking around my condo was a struggle, I didn't even attempt to run or go to work. I ultimately missed several weeks of work, using more than my allotment of sick leave.

Each day that I was sick and unable to train, my Boston qualifying hopes shrank significantly. I finally came to accept that it wasn't going to happen for me in Hartford, and that I'd have to recover from being sick and start a training program all over again. I became frustrated and depressed, and lamented about my situation in my blog.

September 16, 2008

The goal I set for myself nearly a year ago of qualifying for the Boston Marathon this fall is officially washed out. I've now missed over a week due to a virus that I caught during the Virginia Beach Half Marathon. Missing all of this time might have been acceptable back in June or July, but not at this critical stage in training.

My mother and many others have reminded me that my overall health is much more important than running. Somehow, this concept isn't so easy for me to grasp. Really, the main reason I want to be well is to be able to run. I'm more passionate about running than anything else in my life. I don't have a husband or a family like most people my age, so this is what I have devoted my heart to. It's probably hard for non-athletes to understand this passion, but for me, it's been the organizing principle of my life for a long time.

My personality suits me perfectly for running. I'm extremely motivated, goal-oriented, and passionate, with a strong belief in the "effort-result" system. If I work hard at something, it should pay off. I also need structure and control in my life, and running every day provides me with that.

When you live alone, being sick means you don't interact with anyone. Thankfully, my mother came a few times, but aside from that, I've spent way too much time by myself. Which then of course leads to me "thinking" about the situation, and then my life in general, and a complete downward spiral ensues.

I started thinking about how I'll be 30 in less than two months and I'm not happy with how I spent my 20's. I know that you're not "supposed to" have regrets. I don't know what I would have done differently, but I feel like my life has been going in circles and circles for the past 10 years. I'm learning a lot, and I'm growing and changing. But yet my actual lifestyle is the exact same.

I run because it keeps me motivated and it gives me something to look forward to. I feel like I am working toward something every day! There are always new frontiers to reach. New races to experience, new PRs to set. When I can't do that, my whole world feels so pointless. Until I can figure out what major life change I need to make, I have running to keep me going. To keep me moving forward, when everything else in my life just goes in circles and circles.

My one goal for the year (to qualify for Boston) is now down the tubes, and the marathon itself doesn't even look possible at this point. This was the one thing that motivated me every single day—since the moment I registered for the race. And then, just six weeks away when everything was going perfectly, I get hit with a chest virus. Is this supposed to be the grand finale of an entire year's worth of work?

CHAPTER 2:
THE WALL

September 21, 2015

The Boston Athletic Association (B.A.A.) sets qualifying time standards based on age and gender. To be considered for the upcoming 2016 race, women under the age of 35 need to run a marathon in a time of 3:35:00 or faster to qualify. That's an average pace of 8:12 per mile for 26.2 miles. The standards vary by age and gender so that they are equally as challenging for all runners. The standards have also become increasingly difficult in recent years, and just a few years ago, women under the age of 35 could qualify with a 3:40:59 or faster.

Running a qualifying time still does not guarantee someone a spot in the Boston Marathon. Over the years, the race has become so popular that it now fills up immediately when registration opens, and there aren't enough slots for all qualifiers. Today, the qualifying time allows runners to submit a registration, but the B.A.A. will only grant them entry if they are among the fastest runners in their age/gender group that space will permit. There are 30,000 slots, and a portion of those entries are reserved for charity runners. In other words, it's quite competitive to gain entry and therefore extremely prestigious.

I just submitted my application for the Boston Marathon and now I simply have to wait for my confirmation. There's a great deal of speculation about what the cut-off time will be. The B.A.A. announced that registration numbers are up by 15%, but that they weren't necessarily increasing the field size. This means that the race will be more competitive than ever to gain entry into. I'm frankly not surprised. Running has continued to rise in popularity, and now everyone knows someone who's run a marathon. I remember when I first started running marathons, it was considered unique. Few people attempted the 26.2-mile distance. And now, it's probably as common as belonging to a book club, playing a musical instrument, or knitting. Okay—maybe even more common than knitting.

With more and more people running marathons, it's only natural that more and more people will qualify for Boston. Shortly after submitting my application, I check the Boston Marathon Facebook page and a few running forums to listen to the buzz. It sounds like people are sweating pretty hard, thinking that the cutoff time could be significantly lower than it was last year.

"I hope my -2:17 cushion makes it in!" exclaims one of the qualifiers.

"I had been pretty confident about my -2:35 but now I'm not so sure," says another.

I've seen multiple algorithms and fancy calculations trying to predict what this cutoff time will be. In each case, I'm safe with my substantial BQ cushion. There are 5,000 sought-after spots left, and I will be among the first in line to get one. I empathize immensely with the people who are on the borderline. I can't even imagine qualifying for the Boston Marathon by a healthy amount, only to discover months later that my time wasn't fast enough.

I'm not feeling as tortured by this wait as others must be. But part of me won't rest until I see my name on the official entrant list. Even though I've successfully battled my Boston Marathon demons, I still crave this punctuation mark to solidify the achievement.

* * *

On November 11, 2008, I turned 30. Despite my best efforts to celebrate, I wasn't at all happy about my birthday, primarily because I was still single. I had always imagined that I would get married in my late 20's, and instead I was single with no prospects. I lived a solitary life. I had friends, but nobody who I spent time with on a regular basis. I interacted more with my co-workers than anyone else. My parents lived close by and I saw them on the weekends sometimes, but aside from interacting with colleagues at work, my day-to-day was quite lonely.

I filled the void by interacting with people on Myspace, Facebook, and the Runner's World forums. We were entering the world of texting, so picking up the phone and calling someone was starting to become intrusive. I developed closer relationships with my online friends than my "real life" friends, primarily because my online friends shared my interest in running—and that's all I wanted to talk about.

Similarly, I was far more focused on my running career than my marketing career. I was good at my job and I was a high contributor to the company, but the majority of my mental space was occupied with thoughts about running. During my illness, I was worried that my co-workers would think that I was literally running myself into the ground and would become critical of my sport. But instead, everyone was sympathetic.

I led the four-person marketing function for a small software company. I reported directly to the CEO and was responsible for the company's marketing strategy and execution. I liked my job quite a bit. I had been there for nearly three years, which was my longest stint with any company in my 8-year career. It was a small business of about 35 people with a family-like atmosphere and I was given a great deal of creative freedom. Even in the midst of the 2008 recession, the company was doing well and I saw myself staying there for a long time. I expected that the company would grow, and so would my team and the number of marketing initiatives. The job was challenging enough for me to feel mentally active, but not to the point where I needed to work more than 40-45 hours a week. This left me plenty of time to focus on running.

Turning 30 put me in a new age group for races: 30-34 or 30-39 depending on how the race was structured. This didn't change my Boston Marathon qualifying standard, though. It was still 3:40:59, and I'd have to wait until I was 35 for an extra five minutes of leeway.

After mentally rebounding from the illness and dropping out of Hartford, I was focused on plan B. I had chosen the Rock 'n' Roll Arizona Marathon in mid-January as my next race. I continued with the *Advanced Marathoning* program, but made a few minor tweaks here and there to incorporate more speed work. Once again, I was hopeful.

* * *

After several months of preparation, The Rock 'n' Roll Arizona (RNRAZ) Marathon finally arrived and I felt well prepared—far more so than I had been for any previous marathon. Training had gone amazingly well. No illness. No injuries. I was able to follow my plan to the letter. The fact that I had trained so hard and for so long made me think that I was ready to run that elusive 3:40.

In the days leading up to the race, I constantly compared my training for Rock 'n' Roll Arizona to the short training cycle I had for the Shamrock Marathon the previous March. I kept reminding myself of how much fitter I was now than when I ran my 3:51, and also considered all the hard work I had done in the summer of 2008 before I got sick.

Even though I was confident in my training, I was anxious about how the race would turn out. I barely slept the night before the race, mainly because I was worried about the forecast. It was supposed to be "unseasonably warm." *What luck,* I thought, tossing and turning in my hotel bed. *The one year I run Rock 'n' Roll Arizona, it's hot. Usually this race has ideal conditions, but I come to Arizona and the temperature goes way up. It's so unfair.*

Race morning arrived and I was edgy. I was fearful that the heat would wreak havoc on my race. I had been training on a treadmill for the past two months, and I wasn't acclimated to warm weather. To combat the heat and sunshine, I donned a visor, sunglasses, a sports bra (with no shirt), sunscreen, and a running skirt.

Despite my weather angst, I was determined to qualify for Boston and I did not adjust my goal in the slightest. My plan was to go out at a pace of 8:30 and then speed up to goal pace (8:24) by about mile 4. If I could maintain that pace, then my finish time would be about 3:40.

The race started, and I tried to settle into a comfortable rhythm like I had in previous marathons. But this was unlike other marathons—the pressure to perform was more intense. Expectations were higher and there was more on the line. During the third mile, the 3:45 pace group passed me. It seemed as if they were running way too fast to be targeting a 3:45 finish time, so I didn't let it faze me. It did, however, annoy me that this group was now ahead of me, since I was expecting to finish five minutes ahead of them.

I felt "off" during these early miles. My stomach felt a bit heavy because I had overhydrated in the minutes before the race—gulping cup after cup of water. This left me feeling bloated and lethargic. At around mile 7, I finally passed the over-zealous 3:45 pace group and I told myself I would not let them get ahead of me again.

I debated how much water I should drink. It was starting to heat up and the sun was beating down on me. And yet my stomach cramp seemed to be getting worse and worse, and I was beginning to have some upper back pain. I wanted to cross the halfway point at 1:50 or 1:51 because I knew that a lot of people were tracking me, and I wanted my supporters to think I was on target. But as soon as I crossed over the halfway point at 1:51:55, I dramatically slowed down.

I arrived at the mile 14 marker and I hunched over in pain from my stomach cramp. My back was also hurting. Additionally, I was experiencing foot pain. I had felt this same foot pain before in a hot half marathon, so I wasn't terribly worried. I think it was from my foot swelling so much in the heat and then pushing against the top of my shoe. The 3:45 pace group passed me again at this point, and I realized that there would be no way I could BQ. The best I could hope for would be a PR. I was hitting the wall.

In marathon running, "hitting the wall" is something that runners describe as the feeling of needing to stop—as if there is a brick wall in front of you, and you can't possibly go any farther. Usually the wall rears its ugly head at around mile 20 and is the result of insufficient fueling or hydration, or potentially having started the race too quickly.

With my longstanding PR streak, I had never experienced the so-called wall. I was proud of the fact that I was "good" at marathons. Good at pacing, training, fueling, and everything else that went into it. Starting at mile 16 of RNRAZ, the whole race felt like one big brick wall. The foot pain started to get really bad. I sat down on a curb and removed my shoe. The top of my foot was red and swollen, and my big toe felt weird and numb. I eventually put the sock and shoe back on and continued. At this point, I thought I could still feasibly PR if I miraculously got my speed back.

All sorts of negative thoughts ran through my head. Why was I here? Why was I out in the middle of Arizona running 26.2 miles in the heat? Why had I devoted so much of my time and energy to training for this race? What did I want out of my life anyway? Mainly I just wanted to find my life partner and be married. Was all this marathon stuff merely a distraction because I couldn't have what I really wanted? At that point, I felt like someone who was lost in life, trying to find some sense of direction.

By the time I arrived at mile marker 20, I was about 10 minutes off of my target. Any hope I had of a PR was now gone. During mile 22 I sat down on a park bench for about a minute and watched the 3:50 pace group speed by me. I remembered how easy it felt to run with the 3:50 pace group for most of the Shamrock Marathon. I was once in their shoes, running strongly and confidently toward the finish line. And now, despite the fact that I had trained 500% longer and with much greater weekly mileage than I did for Shamrock, I couldn't get my butt off that bench. The heat was zapping me.

Ultimately, I started moving again, but it was a slow, torturous run/walk to the finish line. I reached the 26th mile marker and somehow motivated myself to run that last 0.2 with a smile on my face as I crossed the finish line. At the very least, I thought I could salvage my finish line photo.

My official time was 4:10:55. A few years prior, I would have been elated with that time. But now, I was 30 minutes off of my goal and I was devastated. If my first mistake was expecting that the road to Boston would be a smooth one, my second mistake was allowing myself to wallow extensively in the ditches that I fell into along the way.

January 19, 2009

I've never had a marathon go badly for me. I've run so many of them, and with each one, I've exceeded my goal by a significant amount. And now, after completely revamping my training and putting in so much more time and effort than ever before, I fall so short of my expectations. I did everything "right" this time around, and it's so unfair that this happened to me. I should be celebrating a PR right now!

I definitely don't think I was over-trained. I think I was optimally prepared to BQ, or at least set a significant PR. But I don't deal with heat well—I knew that going into the race. In a way, I feel like I let you all down because I know you were all rooting for me—and then I ended up with this epic failure. After all my talk about how hard I trained and how confident I was about qualifying for Boston, I totally blew it. I guess I'll just have to pull myself back together and crank out the next one.

* * *

I noticed that fewer and fewer people seemed to be active on Myspace and that everyone was moving over to Facebook. This saddened me because I found Myspace to be more of a personal, close-knit community. Facebook didn't have a blog feature and didn't allow users to customize their pages with colors, images, and music. With Myspace, when you went to someone's page, you immediately got a sense of who they were and what they liked. Facebook was more structured, and it wasn't a suitable outlet for expressing my personal thoughts.

Fewer people were reading and commenting on my private Myspace blog and I noticed a rise in "Blogger" blogs, a public platform created by Google. The purpose of my blog was never to have a fan base or a following, but rather to have an outlet of expression. My Myspace subscribers were mainly "Big Cat" runners whom I had met on Myspace, and it wasn't possible to recreate that kind of community elsewhere. Begrudgingly, I transferred my blog over to Blogger because Myspace was becoming obsolete. I named it "Racing Stripes" because I loved zebras and had an unusual fascination with them. I even had a zebra-print running skirt for racing, so the name was quite appropriate.

With Blogger, I had no control over who could see my posts, so I made them less personal. I still talked about my running struggles, but I realized that whatever I wrote could be found by a co-worker or anyone I might start dating. The decline of the Myspace community meant that a large portion of my support network was going away, so I clung more tightly to the Runner's World forums to interact with like-minded people. The problem with this was that I was only interacting with women trying to BQ—I wasn't interacting with a diverse group of runners with different perspectives and motivations for running. This ultimately narrowed my view of running in general, making it seem as if the only reason to run a marathon was to qualify for Boston.

After RNRAZ, my initial instinct was to run another marathon as soon as possible. I had to redeem myself! I actually registered for a small one in Ohio a few weeks later because there was still time to register for the 2009 Boston marathon. But a few days after registering, I realized it probably wasn't a good idea to run another race so soon. I reluctantly gave up hope on Boston 2009 and set my sights on Boston 2010. I also took a step back and reflected more on RNRAZ, and running in general.

February 1, 2009

After having such a miserable experience at the Rock 'n' Roll Arizona Marathon, I didn't think I learned anything. Usually a bad experience can be chalked up to "a learning experience," but I didn't think that was the case with this one. I didn't do anything wrong. I hydrated properly and took in plenty of electrolytes. I tapered properly and I set a goal for myself that was a bit of a stretch, although not unrealistic based on my training. If I had it to do over again, I probably would have started slower. But I had no idea the heat would derail me to such an extent—it's not like I made a bad decision.

Now I can sympathize with people who have bad

marathons. People who hit a wall or bonk. Not because they didn't train properly, but because of the weather or cramping or stomach problems, or whatever. I have had really awful half marathons, but never a bad marathon until just now.

Maybe the lesson is that the more marathons you run, the more likely you are to have bad ones. There's an element of luck involved and there are things that you simply cannot control. When I first started running marathons, my first six were each PRs. It seemed natural that the more of them I did, and the more I trained, the better and better my marathons would get. This is probably true if you look at marathons over several years, but for any one individual race, it's not necessarily true. And maybe the "good ones" that you get are much better than the "good ones" that you had when you first started doing it. But the more you put yourself out there, the more chance you have of things NOT coming together on race day.

I've been really depressed for the last week, and I think the marathon is definitely playing a role. I've never made such a huge investment in terms of time and energy to have it not pay off. Not only did it not pay off—it resulted in the worst marathon I've ever run!

With marathons, you can't just say "that was awful, let me have a do-over tomorrow." It takes time to recover from the marathon, and by the time you do, you've lost some of your fitness. So it takes more time to build up again. And if you want to improve your fitness level even further, it takes even more time to go beyond where you had been. I experienced this when I got sick and had to bail out of the Hartford marathon. I couldn't jump back into training as vigorously as I had been prior to the illness.

I've never been so frustrated with marathoning and training in my whole running career. But that's how it is, and I need to accept this reality if I want to keep at it, and I do. Most people who have run eight marathons can probably cite at least one "bad" race where they were really well prepared but things blew up. Where they had trained hard for months and months, and it ended in a bad experience for them. I'm not any more "cursed" than the next runner.

CHAPTER 3:
GOLDILOCKS

People who don't run typically don't understand the mindset of those who do. Ask a runner why they do it and you'll get a diverse range of answers—there's not one single reason why people train for and run marathons. There are many reasons with a common thread: we feel better about ourselves when we run. More energized, more accomplished, more in shape, more alive, more satisfied, less stressed, less burdened. It's all good stuff.

I existed within a small subset of this growing contingency of runners for whom the flip side was just as strong, if not stronger than the "good stuff" side. Running has made me feel depressed, anxious, defeated, fat, stupid, and trapped. The highs have been high, but the lows have been lower. Because my first six marathons were all PRs, I had no reason to believe that I wouldn't continue to improve. I was completely unprepared for any setbacks, and was unequipped with the coping skills needed to handle disappointment.

* * *

Life got better for me in March 2009. I ran a breakthrough half marathon and I met a man named Greg Clor. At the time, the half marathon was a much bigger deal than a potential love interest.

Running was at the forefront of my mental space and dating was less of a priority. In fact, I hated dating. It was something that felt completely out of my control and had resulted in disappointment more times than I cared to admit. That said, I was extremely lonely and craved a partner in life, so I still tried. I just kept my emotional investment to a minimum.

I met Greg through an online dating site—*Plenty of Fish*. Unlike other sites I had tried in the past, this one was free and fit my mindset of low-investment dating. His profile photo showed him finishing a race, so it naturally caught my eye and I reached out to him. We exchanged a few promising emails, and he seemed more thoughtful and purposeful in his correspondence than anyone I had previously met online. These were characteristics that mattered to me in a man—I was seeking someone who was genuine and expressive and it seemed like Greg might be a good match. His interest in running was a bonus.

I kept my emotions at bay when it came to dating, but became elated when I ran my breakthrough half marathon. I shaved a whopping 4:39 off of my PR from the previous fall, with a finish time of 1:44:04. This race was the first solid indication I had since I started training for Boston that I was getting fast enough to qualify. I had quite a few strong training runs under my belt, but nothing as clear and concrete as this half marathon. It just happened to be the Shamrock Half Marathon—the same race where I had run my fastest full marathon one year prior.

The McMillan calculator, an online tool that estimates equivalent finish times across various distances, indicated that a 3:39:01 was my corresponding marathon time. Given that a 3:40:59 was a BQ, I had nearly two minutes of "wiggle room" based on this race. And I still had nearly two months of training to get even faster before my next full marathon. It seemed as if things were finally turning around for me.

* * *

I had never run the same marathon twice. Part of the allure of the marathon was having varied experiences and seeing different parts of the country and the world. It gave me the opportunity to travel to places that I might never see otherwise. With marathon #9, I broke that rule. I decided to run the New Jersey Marathon for a second time in May 2009. It was a flat course, I had friends who were doing it, it was within driving distance, and the timing worked out well. The weather for the 2007 race had been perfect, and I was hoping for a repeat.

After RNRAZ, I had upped the volume and intensity on my training, averaging 55-60 miles per week. Thankfully, I continued to run injury-free and I felt stronger than ever. I knew I had the speed and endurance needed to hit 3:40—it was simply a matter of actually doing it.

The New Jersey Marathon had nearly doubled in size since I ran it two years prior. Including the marathon, half marathon and relay, the race had about 9000 runners. The city was too small to accommodate all of these people. We were told to park in a satellite lot and take shuttle buses to the start. The buses were an hour late, and I was panicking as I stood there waiting, wondering if I would get to the start on time.

The buses finally arrived all at once and mass confusion ensued as everyone scrambled to get on a bus. Once on board, it was obvious that the drivers didn't know where we were going or where to drop us off. Even though our bus ultimately arrived on time, the race start was delayed by 30 minutes, which meant an extra 30 minutes of standing out in the cold. It was 50 degrees and overcast, and the forecast called for rain, which began shortly after we started running.

My strategy was to run a steady 8:24 pace for the entire duration of the marathon, resulting in a 3:40 finish time. For the first 10 miles, I executed according to plan. The 3:40 pace group was in my sight for these miles, but they were going slightly too fast for my liking, as pace groups tend to do. Everything felt great at this point. It was reminiscent of all my other "good" marathons when the first 10 miles were a walk in the park and I could easily hit the pace with each mile.

I crossed the halfway point in 1:49:49, which was just about perfect. It allowed for a slight slowdown in the second half, but I hadn't made the mistake of starting too fast either. At this point, I realized that I had lost the 3:40 pace group entirely, but I knew they must have been going much faster than they should be.

During the majority of my previous 8 marathons, my

"sweet spot" had been the stretch just past the halfway point, leading up to mile 20. That's when I had typically hit my stride and ran my fastest miles. But during this race, I started to feel tired as I hit mile 14 and even more so at 15. I knew this was a problem and by mile 16, I realized that a BQ was highly unlikely based on how I was feeling.

I figured if I could run sub-9:00's for the rest of the race, I could set a decent PR and maybe run around 3:45. So the notion of a PR kept me going and I kept thinking positive thoughts. I didn't focus on the fact that I would miss the BQ; I just told myself to continue at this easier pace and hold it for the rest of the race.

When I reached mile 20, I realized that I was feeling even worse and that running sub-9:00's for the rest of the race wasn't going to happen. The rain was coming down harder and I wasn't having fun anymore.

I didn't hit an immediate wall like I did in Arizona. Instead, this was a gradual slowdown. It felt wall-ish toward the end because it was so hard, but the most walking I ever did was during mile 25, for maybe about 15 seconds. I was proud of myself for continuing to run, even as the possibility of a PR was slipping away.

All of the runners looked like they were hurting at this point. As much as I was struggling, I was still passing people and I probably looked a lot stronger than I felt. The rain was coming down steadily and I was cold and miserable and not having any fun. I wanted to get to the finish line so badly. I removed my headphones at mile 24 because the music was no longer motivating me.

I looked at my watch as I passed mile 25, and it read 3:39. My ability to do math was completely shot at this point, but I knew that if I ran a sub-10:00 pace for that last 1.2 miles, then I could still get a PR. I knew it would only be by a few seconds, but I needed to salvage this race. I trained too long and too hard to not even get a PR. I was fueled by anger. It had been over a year since I set a marathon PR, despite the fact that the past year of my life had been consumed by marathon training. I needed a PR so badly—I knew how upset I would be if I didn't even get that.

During the last mile I became delirious. A friend from the Runner's World forums who had run the half marathon was cheering for me from a distant parking lot. I recognized her and I screamed back, "Help me! I need you! Help me! I need you!" And I pretty much was saying that for the last quarter mile until I reached the finish line. I knew she couldn't hear me, but for some reason I just kept saying it. I was losing my mind.

I stopped dead in my tracks after crossing the finish line and couldn't take another step. I don't really remember much about what happened next but that all the medical people wanted me to sit down in a wheelchair and I refused. The next thing I knew, I was in the wheelchair anyway being taken to the medical tent. I must have been drifting in and out of consciousness because I don't really remember much about getting into the medical tent.

I heard the EMT guys tell the doctor that I was passing out and that they put me in the wheelchair as I was passing out. I thought to myself that these people were nuts and I was perfectly fine. In my head I felt completely rational and okay, but yet I couldn't talk and couldn't sit up straight.

Soon after, my friend Randi showed up in the medical tent and I called out for her, but I couldn't get her to hear me. Eventually I got her attention, and she came to where I was laying. "Did you BQ?" she asked. I shook my head and frowned, trying to hold back the tears. "Your face is white," she said to me. "And your lips are blue."

The medical people started asking me all sorts of questions and I was not able to properly communicate the answers. It turns out I had hypothermia. My clothing was soaked and I was shivering vigorously. The EMTs said I needed to get out of the wet clothing immediately, but I had nothing dry to change into, and they didn't have anything for me to wear. They gave me a huge blanket, which helped. They wanted me to stay in the medical tent so they could monitor me, but they let me leave under the condition that I would change into dry clothing ASAP. It was still pouring down rain as I exited the tent, and I needed to retrieve my checked bag from the host hotel. It wasn't too far away, but I was struggling to walk. Randi was still in the medical tent, getting treatment for her leg. Some guy saw me shivering and flagged down a cop car to drive me to the hotel. I could hardly move and I couldn't talk, but I ultimately arrived at the host hotel and was able to change into dry clothing.

To add insult to injury, I then had to wait in the pouring rain for about half an hour for the shuttle bus to show up and bring me back to my car in the satellite parking lot. Once again, I was soaking wet and in complete misery about the whole situation. I finally arrived back at my hotel and was able to shower. It was the most glorious shower of my entire life! I must have been in there for an hour trying to thaw out.

Once I was recovered and able to think clearly about the race, the depression set in. I had crossed the finish line in 3:51:09 according to my watch. This was a PR by 40 seconds from the Shamrock Marathon over a year ago. I was relieved that I could officially "claim" a PR and show some amount of progress, but it was no consolation. Boston was still 11 minutes away. At this rate, I wouldn't get my time down to 3:40 for 16 more years!

I called Greg. We'd been on a few dates by that point and he knew how important the marathon was to me. I started telling him about the race, and before I knew it, nearly two hours had passed.

"I'm so upset and frustrated," I lamented. "I trained so hard and I *know* I can run a faster marathon. All I got was an abysmal 40-second PR. And now, I won't be able to run another marathon until the fall."

"You'll get it next time," he assured me. "You can't expect to run your fastest time when it's pouring down rain and you're freezing cold. The fact that you did set a PR in those conditions is pretty remarkable."

Having someone to share my feelings with about my running was amazing. Sure, I had plenty of "running friends" from Myspace and Runner's World to support me, and my mother was always willing to listen. But someone who was willing to hear me drone on and on about a race without getting bored, and even provide a useful perspective—that was pretty incredible. I went to bed feeling hopeful about my future with Greg, but it was overshadowed by the darkness of what I perceived to be a massive failure.

The next day, I wrote a race report in my blog and reflected on all the hard work I'd done over the past year.

May 4, 2009

I feel like Goldilocks and the three bears. "This marathon is too hot!" and then "This marathon is too cold!" From heat exhaustion to hypothermia and nearly a year of training, all I accomplished was shaving 40 seconds off of my marathon time. The whole thing is very disheartening. I know I need a break from marathon training and an "off season," but I want this so badly. I know I can do it. Back when I was setting PRs with each marathon, everything seemed so easy.

I always put 100% of myself into anything that I go after, so it's going to be challenging to back off for the next few months and realize that the BQ probably won't come until December. And even then, I risk the weather being too hot or too cold, or getting sick/injured. It just seems so easy for other people, and I can't seem to get my body to do what I want it to do, and what I know it CAN do.

I know that I ran my best race out there. I trained hard, I pre-hydrated, I tapered, I paced the first half correctly, and then I ran so hard I passed out at the finish. I gunned it at the end when I thought I had nothing left, and managed to squeeze out a 40-second PR. I'm proud of myself for how I ran and how hard I pushed at the end. I'm disappointed with how it all panned out. After a year of hard work, and KNOWING that I am a much better, stronger and faster runner than I ever have been, I can't get a time to reflect that.

I feel defeated, and I feel like the marathon has chewed me up and spit me out. But I love this sport, so I will endure.

* * *

It took me several months to recover mentally from the New Jersey Marathon. I had to step back from running, from my blog, and from the Runner's World forums. Most of the women in my Runner's World group who had set out to BQ the previous summer had already done so, and they began to critique my approach. I was later able to see that these women were not, in fact, critiquing me, but trying to help me out of the misery that I had created for myself. But at the time, I was sensitive to any kind of feedback. I didn't hold it against them, though. I knew they were just trying to help. But I needed to step away from the computer and focus on other aspects of my life. Running was simply too depressing.

Greg and I started dating exclusively that summer, and he moved into a condo across the courtyard from mine. We spent all of our time together and the quality of my life improved dramatically. I was no longer lonely, and Greg (who was training for his first 10-mile race) was supportive and understanding of my struggles with qualifying for Boston.

I also decided it was time to give my training plan a makeover. I purchased the book *Run Faster* by Brad Hudson, read it cover-to-cover and then created a training plan based off of it. I also met up with a local running coach to get some professional feedback on the plan. She thought the plan looked great and advised that I start training by heart rate. To do this, I needed to take a VO2 max test, which would indicate the proper heart rate zones for various workouts.

The test confirmed that I was naturally built for endurance instead of speed, because my body was still working aerobically at a very high percentage of my maximum heart rate. The test also gave me approximate paces for each zone, with my "Lactate Threshold" pace being 7:30, suggesting a marathon pace of around 8:15. The test administrator told me that physiologically, running a 3:40 marathon was completely feasible for me, and that I could probably even run a 3:35 in good conditions.

One of the best things about heart rate training was that I didn't have to worry about my training paces. As long as I stayed within the prescribed heart rate zone I knew I was getting the maximum fitness benefit. On the other hand, it was just another data point to obsess over.

PART II

AN OBSESSION

CHAPTER 4:
CONTROL

People often ask me how I got into running. The short answer is that I started running a few months after graduating college as a way to stay in shape. The long answer is much more complicated.

The long answer is that shortly after graduating college in 2000, my life fell apart and I needed something positive to focus on. I was laid off from my first job out of college, my love life was one disaster after another, my parents were recently divorced and remarried, I was living alone for the first time ever, and I seemed to be drifting apart from many of my friends.

In an attempt to make things better for myself, I turned my focus to fitness. I joined a nearby gym for the primary purpose of taking step aerobics classes. It was the closest thing to dance I could find, and I had danced since the age of three. Along with my membership came a free body fat assessment. At 5'5" and 120 pounds, I was told that I had 30% body fat, which was unhealthy.

Initially, I shrugged it off. Never in my life did I have body image issues and I wasn't about to start. But when I began to get really depressed with my life in January of 2001, I decided I would make a concentrated effort to get in shape and lower my body fat percentage. The more I focused on it, the more energized and upbeat I felt. Finally, I had a goal that was entirely within my control. Things like having a good job or a romantic relationship were not within my control, but lowering my body fat percentage was.

Because I didn't have a body fat monitor at home, the only indication I had of progress was the scale. And I had also come to equate healthy eating with low-calorie eating. I tried to educate myself on nutrition (something that I had never focused on in my life), and pretty much everything I read talked about calories. Calories were the enemy when trying to be healthy (at least that's what the magazines said), so I began to strictly control my intake.

That's where running came in. My step aerobics class was only offered twice a week so I supplemented it with treadmill running. The treadmill had a handy little "calories burned" indicator on it, and I loved watching that number go up and up the more I ran.

When I lost my first five pounds I felt amazing! Victory! I finally was able to achieve something all on my own. I owned my accomplishment outright. I received positive reinforcement from my family and friends that I was now embracing a healthy lifestyle. I had dramatically changed my diet, cutting out all fried foods, beef, pork, cheese, chips, and most sweets. I started buying "diet" versions of all foods. The fewer the calories, the better. I logged every calorie I ate, and subtracted every calorie that I burned on the treadmill. This resulted in a steady weight loss over the course of several months. Prior to this point in my life, I didn't even know what a calorie was.

When I lost another five pounds (down to 110) I was elated, and I realized that I didn't need to lose any more weight. However, this weight loss thing had become a way of life for me. It's all I thought about. Food, weight, and calories were constantly on my mind. Instead of feeling sad and depressed for the state that my life was in, I had something to focus on that was entirely within my control. As long as I was losing weight nothing else mattered, I was satisfied.

Even though I didn't actively try to lose any more weight, I found myself afraid to eat any more and run any less than I had been previously. In fact, when I ate un-planned for calories (like someone leaving a piece of pie on my desk at work) I felt horribly guilty. So much so, that after that slice of pie, I ran up and down the stairwell at work to counteract the sinful dessert. I'd go out with my friends and eat more than I felt comfortable with, and immediately go to the gym afterwards (even if it was late at night) to run off the calories. With every mile that I ran, I felt less and less anxious, and as the "calories burned" counter rose, I felt more at peace with myself.

Eating disorders exist because they work. They serve a purpose, and for me that purpose was to achieve something entirely within my control. It made the stuff that was not in my control (like my love life) much easier to accept.

At 100 pounds, I knew my weight was low enough that I could no longer deny I had a problem. I didn't *want* to be anorexic. But the idea of gaining weight seemed scary to me. Even though I had been perfectly content with my body at higher weights (at every stage on the way down), 100 pounds felt like a hard-earned accomplishment. And I didn't want to give it up. I finally admitted that I had a problem to my family and friends and sought help from a therapist. However, the therapist I found was completely useless, even though she supposedly specialized in eating disorders, and I fared much better through online support groups.

My weight was up and down for years, transitioning from "anorexic" to "underweight," but never getting back into the "healthy weight" category. I tried to let go of my need to be at a low weight, but it was difficult to do so.

I continued treadmill running. I actually really liked my time on the treadmill. I would make running playlists, enjoy the music, and feel good about pushing the pace. I built up some speed and endurance, typically running 5-6 miles a day. I also lifted weights, as this was something that the original personal trainer told me would get my body fat down.

I discovered road racing in 2005 when I ran a 2-mile race at my college reunion. I won the race outright and it felt amazing. The following weekend, I ran a 10K in Washington DC and was elated to see that I was in the top 25% of all the women. From there, I moved on to the half marathon, and finally my first marathon in the spring of 2006. During this time, I decided that fueling my runs and being psychically healthy was much more important than my weight, so I started to eat more. Eventually, the eating disorder faded into the background and I was able to eat without guilt most of the time. My weight stabilized at the bottom of the "healthy" range, and I became more focused on my race times than the number on the scale.

In trying to overcome my eating disorder, I had gained quite a bit of self-awareness. I knew that I was a black-and-white thinker, that I was a perfectionist, and that I thrived off of accomplishments. I knew that my eating disorder was never about body image, but rather a way to numb out negative emotions and feel in control of my life. I had "worked on myself" to the extent that I could without the help of an effective therapist. I had no more symptoms of an eating disorder and food no longer haunted me. Instead, I was focused on running. On the surface, this seemed much healthier. But peeling back the layers revealed that it was not, in fact, *that* much healthier from a mental perspective.

With a prolonged period of no improvement to my marathon time, and multiple failed attempts to qualify for Boston, I began to feel like an anorexic who had lost her ability to lose weight. The one area of my life that I felt like I could control—the one goal that I thought I could achieve without anyone's stamp of approval—now was no longer in my control. And it tortured me.

* * *

My next target race was the Toronto Waterfront Marathon in late September. My training that summer had gone exceptionally well. I enjoyed the novelty and variety of my training plan and Greg started to join me for some of my runs. My weekly mileage was higher than it ever had been, and I logged my first 60-mile week. Needless to say, I felt extremely fit. But as every runner knows, injury is most likely to strike when you are at your fittest.

August 31, 2009

A few days ago, during an easy treadmill run, I suddenly felt a pain on the outside of my foot. I kept running in the hopes that it would go away, but it didn't, so I stopped after five miles instead of the planned six. I limped my way off of the treadmill, and my foot has been hurting ever since.

Now it's Monday and it still hurts to walk on my foot. I've been swimming and using the elliptical machine (neither seem to irritate it), but that is no substitute for running. I just want to maintain what I have. At this point, I am not looking to gain more fitness, but I also don't want the past 8 weeks of hard training to come undone. I can't predict when it will get better—all I can do is keep resting my foot and taking care of it. I'll go back to my physical therapist on Friday.

I cried a lot on Saturday. It hurt to walk on my foot, so every step was a reminder that I was injured. I couldn't put it out of my mind. Greg even carried me a few blocks in D.C. on our way to dinner because it hurt with every step, and I could only walk slowly.

Maybe it's not meant to be. Maybe I am not meant to qualify for Boston. I always come so close, and then something comes along at the last minute to ruin it. It never works for me, and it's always a matter of bad luck. I do everything in my power to train smart but the "stars" don't align for me.

Greg says that if there weren't obstacles to qualifying for Boston, then it wouldn't be worth attaining. That's what makes it all the sweeter—having to overcome obstacles and fight for it. I agree with this, but I also feel like I have faced more than my fair share of obstacles. And I see so many people train for one season, run the marathon, and get the time they worked for. Heck, I used to do that, too—back before I set my sights on Boston.

* * *

Unfortunately, I was not able to run for about five weeks, which meant no Toronto Waterfront Marathon. The foot injury left me feeling severely depressed, and I was grateful that Greg was there to help me through it. At one point, after not having run on it for three weeks, I went for a "test run" on the track to see if my foot was any better. Much to my dismay, it started hurting almost instantly. I returned to Greg's condo (we essentially lived together since our condos were so close) and waited for him to come home.

He found me crying in his bed, and to this day he reminds me how surprised he was to find me there in that state.

"My run was horrible," I cried. "My foot still hurts! I'm missing so much training! There's no way I'm going to be able to run Toronto. And then I'm going to have to spend so much time working to rebuild everything I've lost."

"I'm so sorry, honey," he said, as he embraced me. "I was thinking about you during my treadmill run and really hoping your foot would be better."

"Me too. I can't fucking believe this is happening to me. AGAIN. It's going to be forever until I qualify for Boston."

"I realize you're upset, and you have every right to be," he replied, patiently. "But I really think you should get out of this bed and continue on with the weekend. We have so many things to do—you don't want to spend the day in bed, do you?"

Despite Greg's best efforts to bring me back into the land of the normal, I remained depressed for quite a while. Post after post in my blog told one long sob story.

October 6, 2009

One of the worst things about a running injury is that when every step hurts, it's a constant reminder that you can't run. You can't just shove it into the back of your mind and focus on other things. Every step says, "You're injured and you can't run." I am extremely upset that after training so hard all summer, everything has blown up in my face.

It seems like it's so easy for everyone else. Greg and I recently went to a wedding and we were chatting with some of the other guests. The conversation turned to running and the woman said she just ran her first marathon not too long ago. Her husband chimed in, "Yeah, and she qualified for something." The woman looked back at me and said, "I had no idea, but afterwards I was told that I qualified for another marathon. I'm probably not going to do it, but that was cool." Of course I smiled and congratulated her, but inside I wanted to throw stuff at her.

I'm happy for all of my friends who have been setting PRs left and right this year, but at the same time, it just frustrates me even further because I have only had one good race in 2009—a half marathon. Now that the fall racing season has kicked into high gear, I am seeing so many people run amazing races, and I am not even able to participate. I know that if I did, I would run some of my slowest times ever.

My spirit is really drained from all of this. I've had so many strong training cycles and something always comes along to mess up my BQ. I think I've had the physical ability to qualify for Boston for the past year, and yet I haven't managed to run a marathon that wasn't sabotaged by weather or illness or injury. My half marathon from March, my VO2 max test, and my training all indicate that I could have run a 3:35 or faster in Toronto. I have to keep reminding myself that my day will come, but I am getting so discouraged that I am starting to think that training doesn't even matter.

CHAPTER 5:
EXPECTATIONS

The word "obsession" has all the letters in it that you'd need to spell Boston, except for the T. But the T is so powerful that it can have its own word: "time." Time Obsession. That's what Boston was for me, and it's what I thought it needed to be in order to get there. If you're not 100% focused on the goal at all times, then how can you hope to achieve it?

Where do you draw the line between having a goal that you work toward every day—that affects how you plan your life and everything you do—and an obsession? Is obsession unhealthy? To be great at something, don't you need to be obsessed? No. In fact, I would learn that just the opposite is true.

I clung to my race times and workout paces so closely because they were objective. The clock didn't lie or discriminate. With time as the key metric, I always knew exactly where I stood and there are no grey areas. What's more—I felt like my race times were something that I could control, and I therefore expected myself to do so. I expected that by putting in the training, I would be able to significantly reduce my marathon time.

Anything that interfered, like the weather, illness, or injury was nearly impossible for me to accept because hey—I controlled my own running times! I've learned that with running, and with all things in life, accepting the things that I cannot control and focusing on the things that I can is the key to a healthy mindset and ultimately, success. In terms of expectations, I now expect myself to run to the best of my ability, regardless of the circumstances. And the "best of my ability" does not always equate to a PR.

* * *

The northern Virginia area got hit with a record-breaking amount of snow in January 2010. Greg and I were snowed into our condos for days at a time, on multiple occasions. He had proposed to me the previous Thanksgiving, and being snowed in was a nice preview of our future life together. Whenever I felt depressed about my BQ failures, I reminded myself that I had what really mattered most in life—a man who truly loved me whom I would spend the rest of my life with.

Even with mounds of snow everywhere, the gym was within walking distance and I was able to train on a treadmill. There were two weekends when I drove to a park about 30 minutes away from my condo because it was the only area I knew of that was plowed.

I proceeded with the same training plan that I used the previous summer, although with slightly lower mileage to avoid another foot injury. I could tell that I was getting faster and fitter based on the paces I was running in my workouts, which corresponded to the correct heart rate zones. In other words, I wasn't over-running my workouts according to my heart rate; I had simply reached a new fitness level. I discovered that I loved running in cold temperatures, with the 30's being perfect for long runs.

Given my successful training cycle, I fully expected that I would qualify for Boston at the upcoming Shamrock Marathon. I had had great "luck" at Shamrock for each of the past two years (the full marathon in 2008 and the half marathon in 2009), so naturally I was optimistic that things would go well.

My outlook changed entirely when the weather forecast came out, calling for temperatures in the mid to upper 60's with sunny skies. The day before the race, while walking around outside in 70-degree weather, tears started flowing down my face. Everyone else seemed so happy and excited about the race and yet there was a huge cloud hanging over me. After training through snow and ice all winter long, I was greeted with warm and sunny weather on race day. It was so unfair!

I tried so hard to be positive, but my logic made that impossible. I even made a list of things that were going to be different from RNRAZ. For example, there was no time zone change. I also had an extra year's worth of training under my belt, and I knew I was much faster and fitter than ever before. But realistically, I knew that I wasn't likely to BQ in such unseasonably warm weather.

On race morning, I headed to the start with a positive outlook. I was calm and I was determined to do my best. I wore sunglasses, a visor, my sports bra and a running skirt. No headphones. Even though I enjoyed running with music during my previous marathons, the last thing I needed in this weather was another piece of equipment weighing me down.

I started off at a pace of 8:25 and it felt ridiculously easy. It was short lived, however, once I came to an area that was un-shaded and the sun was rising higher in the sky. Things started to get tough during the 9th mile, but I held the pace anyway. At mile marker 10, I felt like I was racing at half-marathon effort instead of full marathon effort, but I maintained the pace anyway. By the time I reached mile marker 11, I knew that my race was over. It all happened very quickly. I didn't feel uncomfortably hot—I just became extremely tired and exhausted. I slowed down to a 9:00 pace, and then to a 9:15 pace. Swarms of people started passing me and I simply couldn't keep up. I wanted to stop after mile 11, but I knew that Greg was waiting for me shortly after the halfway point.

I continued on and I saw some friends from the Runner's World forums after mile 12. I stopped running to hug them and I realized how horrible I felt. I don't think I could even communicate properly at that point. I felt like I might pass out. I resumed running, but it was more like a "survival shuffle" at this point.

When I finally saw Greg, I stopped running and pulled off the course. I could barely even talk to him. He pulled me over into a shaded area and sat me down on the ground. He had water, a bag of ice, a cookie and a granola bar with him. I hung out there for about 30 minutes before I felt ready to walk back to the hotel. Once again, I was devastated.

March 22, 2010

This is the first marathon out of 10 that I Did Not Finish (DNF). At mile 11, when I was coming to terms with the fact that my race was doomed, I asked myself if I would regret it if I stopped. And the answer was an immediate no. I knew that one of these three things would happen:

1) I would continue to push at an 8:25 pace and pass out.
2) I would run/walk to the finish like I did in Arizona with a mediocre time and then not recover for 3-4 weeks.
3) I would stop at mile 13.5 and cut my losses.

I chose the third option and had no regrets. If it hadn't been for Arizona, then perhaps I would have continued. But I had learned a valuable lesson in Arizona—my body has limitations in sunny weather. Even in the 50's and 60's where many runners are absolutely fine, I simply don't tolerate it. If I had Arizona to do over again, I would have stopped at the halfway point. I wasn't about to make the same mistake twice.

The tough thing for me is that I am so much less heat tolerant than the average runner. No one else was slowing down so early in the race. I even "bonked" at the Cherry Blossom 10-miler (at mile 6) last year when it was sunny and 55. When I told my runner friends that it was too hot and sunny for me, it was hard for them to believe. Sunny and 55 are ideal race conditions for a lot of people.

As I was slowing down, another runner encouraged me to keep going. I said that I was not going to finish. He said, "Walk if you have to. Just do whatever it takes to finish the race." I completely disagree with this. Granted, he didn't know me or my marathon history. But why would I kill myself to make it to the finish line of a marathon that I have already completed, only to do it slower and then be beat up for the next three weeks? What would I gain? I would have hated myself for making such a poor choice. And this is if I even made it that far and didn't pass out before getting there.

The bottom line is that I know what my body can and can't handle. My limitations with regards to sunny/warm weather are greater than those of other runners. I should not attempt to run a marathon in conditions that make it impossible to meet my goal, especially considering how much time and effort I put into training. I really thought I would be safe with a March 21 marathon, but apparently I was not.

What upsets me most is that I have not had a positive marathon experience in over two years. And the irony of this is that my fitness level has significantly improved during this time period. My last good marathon was at Shamrock in 2008. Ever since then there has been a major illness, an injury, two cases of heat exhaustion and one case of hypothermia. My first 7 marathons were so wonderful. I just want to experience that joy again.

* * *

It was a busy spring. Greg and I bought a house together and continued planning for our August wedding. Our house was a foreclosure, so we had the entire place re-painted and re-floored before moving in. One of the best things about the new house was that Greg and I could run outside safely and not be in the middle of a construction zone—we could leave directly from our front door and run through local neighborhoods. At the condos, we had to drive to a trail or use a treadmill because the immediate area surrounding us wasn't safe for running. Now, I could do 100% of my runs outdoors, and never have to run on a treadmill.

In April, I ran a breakthrough 5K. I had been stuck at around 23:30 for three years, and I shocked myself with a 22:21 at a local evening race. Even though my intense marathon training wasn't making my marathon time budge, it was nice to see a significant PR at a shorter distance. I knew I was getting fitter and faster; I just needed my marathon luck to improve.

My plan for the fall was to run the NYC Marathon with Greg, as it would be his first. I wanted to prioritize having that experience with him over trying to qualify for Boston. This meant that if I wanted to qualify for the 2011 race, I needed to run another marathon that same spring. The Potomac River Run marathon was a small local race scheduled six weeks after Shamrock. I thought that would give me enough time to recover and ramp up again. I knew I risked the weather being warm in an early May race, but that was the most feasible option.

A few days before the race, the forecast came out and it called for temperatures in the mid 60's with high humidity. I had learned from Shamrock that these were not conditions that I could BQ in, so I registered for yet another marathon two weeks later that some of my Runner's World friends were doing. The other marathon was also small and it was only a two-hour drive. It was called the Bob Potts Marathon.

Since I had registered for Potomac River, I figured I would run the first half of it as a training run and then stop. The halfway point was back at the start line, so it would be easy for me to run 13 miles and then drive home. It would give me good practice being in a race setting, and I'd have the advantage of water stations and people cheering. My plan was to run it at my typical long run pace (about 9:15-9:30) and then stop after 13 miles.

That morning, I woke up, got dressed, took one Honey Stinger gel from the pantry as well as a water bottle and headed out. When I got to the race, I started chatting with other runners. I told them that my plan was to go halfway, and maybe a few miles after that if I felt okay. I told them about how I wanted to qualify for Boston, and I knew it wasn't going to happen in this weather, so I was going to wait two weeks for the Bob Potts Marathon.

May 2, 2010

The race started at 6:00 in the morning. It was an out-and-back course on the C&O Canal Towpath—times two. My plan was to run one of the out-and-backs (13.1 miles) as a training run, keeping my heart rate in the easy range. Here's the play-by-play.

1- 8:42 Lots of women are passing me. That's okay.
2- 8:37 Nicely done.
3- 8:42 I stop at a water station for about 1 minute and chat with one of the volunteers.
4- 8:55 A tree branch is blocking the course, so I decide to move it out of the way for everyone.
5- 8:44 I'm back to running again, keeping my heart rate in the easy zone.
6- 8:40 Still in the easy zone, and I am passing people!

7- 8:36 The girl I just passed is completely out of breath—I wonder if she'll make it the whole way.
8- 8:51 Yay, I passed another woman!
9- 8:33 Wow, I can't believe it's already been 9 miles.
10- 8:30 Oooh, someone just told me I was the "first chick."
11- 8:26 Maybe I will speed up a bit!
12- 8:48 Damn, this still feels easy.
13- 8:26 I could stop and get a 1:52 half marathon, but I want to turn around and keep running.
14- 8:21 I feel great! Maybe I can BQ. I only need to average about 8:02 for the rest of the race.
15- 8:03 Yes, I can BQ!
16- 8:18 Well ... maybe I'll just go for being the first female
17- 8:16 I'll end up with a 3:44 which will still be awesome. I'm gonna go for it!
18- 8:31 Actually, I am getting tired, probably should drop out, I want a BQ, and I'm willing to sacrifice a PR for it.

I ran a total of 18.5 miles at an average pace of 8:33, and I was the first female by about three minutes. I stopped at the water station and the volunteers asked me if I was okay. I was perfectly fine, but I told them my dilemma: PR today, or BQ in two weeks? None of them knew what to tell me. I called Greg using one of the volunteer's cell phones. I told him my dilemma. He didn't know what to say. I told him I would run for a bit longer and potentially finish the race.

I started running again, but then turned right back around and decided to stop. I realized that my legs were tired, and if I went for it, my legs wouldn't be recovered in time for the Bob Potts Marathon. Additionally, I had done a 10-mile progression run two days prior, and I thought my legs would feel that starting at mile 20. Plus, I only had one Honey Stinger gel. That's not enough fuel for a marathon.

I received an interesting comment on this blog post:

Was it the sun or was it the fact that you didn't place any pressure on yourself for this day? Sounds like the race might be more in your head. Go out and have fun! Stay positive and don't focus on

the BQ focus on that day that minute. Know in your heart and head
how strong you are and you'll get that BQ when the stars all line
up. If they aren't aligned in two weeks so what, you might just
finish first!

I didn't think too much about his comment. I knew that ideally I
wouldn't place so much pressure on myself, but I wanted this BQ
so badly—I didn't know how NOT to feel pressured. Even when I
tried to relax and tell myself it was just for fun, I knew that I was
lying to myself.

The Potomac River Marathon demonstrated that I could, in
fact, run well in less-than-ideal conditions. Instead of focusing on
that as my takeaway, I focused on the fact that I was in great shape
and therefore more determined than ever to qualify for Boston.
Instead of reducing the pressure I would put on myself at Bob
Potts, I raised my expectations because I knew what I was
physically capable of.

This was my third mistake on the road to Boston—setting
"outcome-based" expectations that were not entirely within my
control. I would have fared much better to set expectations of the
"process" running the race. As with most things in life, results and
outcomes are not entirely within our control. Getting a job, for
example, requires someone else's stamp of approval. Even
something that seems objective, like a multiple-choice test, isn't
entirely controllable unless you can predict the exact questions
ahead of time. If you expect certain outcomes that aren't within
your control, you're likely setting yourself up for disappointment.

* * *

May 16, 2010

Today wasn't what I expected it to be. After waiting over a year
since my last marathon to try again, I was really expecting to blow
it out of the water with a 3:35. Even so, my strategy was to start
out conservatively (slower than BQ pace) and then negative split.

All the signs pointed to a BQ (3:40) being attainable, with
something like 3:35 being perfectly realistic.

1. In March 2008, I ran a 3:51:49. This was based on a 7-

week training cycle, averaging about 40 miles per week. Since then, I have had quite a few marathon training cycles, each one peaking at 55 miles per week or more, and each one at least 12 weeks in length. I would expect significant improvement based on this training.

2. In March 2009, I ran a half marathon at 1:44:04. This predicts a marathon from 3:37-3:40, depending on whose calculator you use. This was over a year ago, and my fitness level has increased significantly since then, and I have continued to train with weekly mileage in the 40s and 50s.

3. Most recently, I ran a 5-miler in 37:10 and a 5K in 22:21. Both of these races predict times faster than 3:40. Although one could argue that you can't predict marathon times based on these calculators, I have always found my longer races (half marathons and full marathons) to be "faster" than their equivalent shorter races. In other words, endurance is my strength. My body works aerobically at a higher percentage of max heart rate than most people, which correlates to better performance in longer races.

4. Two weeks ago, I ran 18.5 miles at an average 8:33 pace, and I had sped up during the last five miles to an 8:20 pace. I felt great, and I thought I could have continued at a 8:33 pace or faster for at least another 3-4 miles. This was despite the heat (in the 70's) and humidity.

I went into this race with a great deal of confidence. I wasn't sick or injured, and the weather was reasonable. It was in the mid 50's and overcast at the start and rose to the low 60's and sunny at the end. These aren't ideal conditions for me, but they are decent, and I didn't think they would make me bonk.

I started out at a very controlled pace. I reached the halfway point at 1:51:45, which is slower than BQ pace. I knew that the first half was a net uphill and the second half was a net downhill, so I did this purposely. I figured that I could easily log 8:10's on the way back and smash the BQ. Only that's not what happened.

Things did get much easier after the halfway point, and I logged an 8:16, 8:22, and 8:17. But after that, I could feel myself starting to fade. 8:17 became 8:30 became 8:40 became 9:00 and so on. I knew at mile 16 that I wasn't going to keep the pace I needed to BQ, but I was still hopeful about a nice PR. This is very similar to how I felt in New Jersey last spring.

By mile 18, I was miserable. I was in so much pain and I didn't know why it got so hard for me. I was well hydrated (carried a bottle for most of the race), took plenty of gels, etc. I was a bit suspicious of that 18.5 miler two weeks ago, but that seriously felt "easy." Even still, I don't think that any of this really explains what happened out there. I am in so much better shape than I was two years ago and yet I couldn't even beat that time!

In complete agony (both physical and mental), I crossed the finish line in 3:53:55. I do think this is a respectable time, but nowhere near what I am capable of. Greg was waiting for me at the end, and I knew he understood exactly what I was going through. I didn't need to say a word. I was in shock, I was drained, I was in pain—I felt broken in so many ways. I didn't speak for a good 10 minutes. I regretted not having gone for the PR two weeks ago. I felt stupid. I felt I had sacrificed so much for this one goal, and I didn't even come close.

I started crying. I felt so crushed, so defeated, and so ashamed for having been so cocky. Guilty, even, for having solicited the support of so many of my runner friends. And that I let them down. The race director approached me and asked me how I did—I just looked at him with tears in my eyes and said that I didn't do it. Everything I have worked so hard for. . . it's all came down to this.

Maybe there was a higher power at work trying to teach me something by not letting me BQ or PR. Part of the reason I wanted this so badly was to cross it off my list and move on. I've been obsessing about it throughout my entire engagement and it's overshadowed the happiest time of my entire life! I guess what I've learned is that BQ or no BQ, I need to change my focus. I am extremely motivated and goal-oriented—and it typically "works" in terms of achieving what I want to achieve. But for some reason, not in this case. And I think that reason is that I need to see the bigger picture of my life, appreciate what I have, and focus on all the wonderful changes.

As with all of my best races, it will come when I least expect it to. The week before I ran my 3:51 back in 2008, I thought I was seriously injured. I thought I'd probably have to drop out at mile 5. But instead, I exceeded my goal. When I ran the Houston half marathon in 2008, I had been injured for three weeks, and I expected a 2:00 "fun run." Instead, I PRed with a 1:50. It was completely unexpected. Two weeks ago, I wasn't even trying to run a marathon, but I ran a good percentage of it at an awesome pace given the weather conditions. When I least expected it.

From now on I think I need to go into races with no expectations. I should know where I am fitness-wise and what to target, but ultimately, I need to realize that every race is a gamble, an unknown. No matter how much training you do or how great you feel, the race could still be miserable. Or, no matter how badly you feel or how unprepared you are, you could rock it! I put far too much pressure on myself, and from now on I am going to back off and let it happen. With that approach, do I worry that I won't be as motivated to train? A little. But I know I will be more balanced if I keep a more laid-back approach to this whole thing.

CHAPTER 6:
PATIENCE

September 23, 2015

Now, as I await my official Boston Marathon acceptance, I realize that I am not alone in my journey. Thousands of other people have reached this place, and each one of them has a unique story. Today I saw a post from the Boston Marathon in my Facebook newsfeed around noon stating that not all applicants would be granted an entry. Only the fastest qualifiers will be accepted. I've known this for a long time, but I am still fascinated by the idea of actual Boston qualifiers not being able to run the race.

The Facebook comments on that post were heart wrenching. So many Boston Marathon hopefuls are wondering if their qualifying "buffer" is large enough to grant them an entry. I scrolled through the comments, and realized that behind every Boston Marathon qualifier, there is a story:

"It's torture waiting, but I know the B.A.A. is doing their best. I DO think this is the most fair way, and if my cushion of 2:35 isn't good enough, so be it. Tears could be shed, but my running shoes will go back on the next day to train harder."

"I will be heartbroken, but I also chose this sport and Boston is something I choose to go after. I really want to run it, but in the

end it is up to me to get myself to that level, I am proud I qualified and know that even if it is not this year, I will run Boston one day."

"I have a 3:35:51 and BQ-4:09. Logic says we're good. But my gut is still churning."

"It's stressful waiting. This is my first time to qualify. I've been trying for 19 years and it's finally happened. I was actually tearing up yesterday while filling out the registration form."

"I just want to know the cutoff so I can get some sleep."

I empathize deeply. But I cannot spend the next week tormented by this. I know my qualifying cushion is large enough, so I just need some patience. Patience is a skill, and it's one I've been forced to learn.

* * *

After the Bob Potts disaster, I realized I needed a mental break from trying to qualify for Boston. It was destroying my overall wellbeing. I realized how obsessed, anxious, and depressed I became before and after each attempt, and I didn't want all that negativity to overshadow all of the good things in my life.

Greg I and I got married on August 14, 2010. We incorporated running into our wedding by laminating our old bib numbers and using them as table numbers. Instead of tables 1-10, we had tables 5634, 305, etc. It was a fun and creative way to express something that we both enjoyed.

My next marathon would not be a qualifying attempt. I planned to run the New York City Marathon alongside Greg. It would be his first marathon and I wanted to share the experience with him. I obtained a charity entry for the race, pledging to raise $3,000 for the Central Park Conservancy. My primary focus was simply to enjoy running with Greg. I determined that the BQ would be out of sight and out of mind for a while.

October 13, 2010

I was obsessed with qualifying for Boston for two years. I ate, drank and slept Boston and the magical 3:40 that would get me there. Despite my strong training and significant PRs in other distances, I haven't gotten my marathon time down in over two years.

So, back in May, after my most recent failed attempt, I just said "F" it. I wanted to focus on my upcoming marriage and my life with my husband. So, this time I have taken a much more relaxed approach. I wrote my own training program and I have been very loosely following it—usually re-arranging it based on how my body feels. Most of my runs have been with my husband. I wrote his plan as well and he's been following it practically to the letter. My goal in NYC is not to run the best race I can, but to enjoy the incredible experience that is NYC with my new husband—supporting him in his first marathon.

Even though I wasn't trying to qualify for Boston, I still felt like there was a monkey on my back. Like I had set out to do something and put a great deal of time and effort toward it, but with no result. Whenever I told people that I ran marathons, they'd often reply, "Have you run Boston?" Why was that so frequently the next question? Couldn't it just be that I had run a lot of marathons, period?

Runners and non-runners alike would ask me this question, and I wanted to scream whenever it came up. In my mind, this was the conversation:

Other person: What do you do for fun?
Me: I run marathons.
Other person: How many have you run?
Me: About 10.
Other person: Wow. Have you run the Boston Marathon?
Me: Not yet.
Other person: Oh.

My translation of the other person's "oh" was: "You said you've run so many marathons that I thought you would have done Boston by now. But I guess not." I always assumed that others were as critical about my running as I, myself, was. I wanted to not care, to not focus on Boston. But it was always there in the background.

Meanwhile, I did manage to set a significant half marathon PR that fall. Even though I thought that my 1:44:04 PR from Shamrock 2009 was strong, I was confident that I could run a faster half marathon, given all of the training I was doing for NYC.

I had signed up for a local race 20 minutes away from my house. I raced as hard as I could and ended up with a 1:41:40—a PR by over two minutes. I also won third place in my age group, which was icing on the cake. I relished my achievement, which was further "proof" that I was actually getting fitter, despite my marathon time not budging.

* * *

The NYC Marathon gave both Greg and me a new respect for the 26.2-mile distance. It was the most challenging marathon course I had ever run, and I underestimated how much the hills would take out of us. We started out strong, but things fell apart in the later miles for both of us, and we wound up running a 4:08:32. Given that this was Greg's first marathon, I was proud of him. He was just happy to have finished, but was not expecting so much pain during the last eight miles. It was nice to run a marathon "for fun" again, without the pressure of a BQ looming over my head. The day was about experiencing something new with my husband, and we enjoyed it.

Four weeks later, it was time for the St. Jude Memphis Marathon. I had suggested that my company sponsor the race as a way of getting more involved with the charity, and they agreed. Several people from my company flew down to Memphis for the event.

My plan for the race was to run it at 100% effort, but not to attempt to qualify for Boston. In other words, I wanted to run somewhere between a 3:40 and my PR of 3:51. Given that I had just run NYC four weeks earlier, I knew my legs were likely not fully recovered, so a BQ would be highly unlikely.

December 5, 2010

The St. Jude Memphis Marathon was not a target race for me. In fact, I wasn't even sure if I would run the full marathon based on how torn up I felt after NYC—I had the option of running the half marathon instead. But I felt strong enough to run the full, so I decided to go for it. I wasn't trying to BQ, but I felt like I was a shoo-in for a PR, given my recent half marathon time.

The weather was 54 and overcast. I was happy to have an overcast day, but 54 degrees was about 10 degrees higher than I would have liked. I thought that as long as the sun didn't come out, the weather shouldn't hold me back too much.

The early miles were relatively crowded, given that both the half and the full marathoners were on the same course. My strategy was to walk through the water stations to prevent leg fatigue later in the race. I did this in my marathon back in March of 2008, so I figured it would work again. I really didn't want to bonk and I wanted to play it conservatively. For these early miles, I ran in the 8:30-8:45 range, depending on the hills. I hit the 10K point at 53:37, which is an 8:39 pace. There seemed to be an equal amount of uphill and downhill, and I ran based on effort. It felt very easy, but I kept telling myself that it should feel really easy so early in the race.

Miles 8-10 took us on a path through the woods, and it was quite hilly. In fact, it seemed as if this entire segment was uphill, and I did not want to overdo it early in the race. I crossed the halfway mark in 1:54:30, which is a pace of 8:45. During all of my previous BQ attempt bonks, I had reached the halfway point in 1:50 or faster. So I knew I had conserved energy, and set myself up for a smart race.

Miles 14-20 were a steady uphill climb, with no downhills to be found. This was very disheartening to me because I was hoping that after a conservative first half, I'd be able to speed up during the second half, but I was still running in the 8:50-8:55 range on these hills. And by mile 18, I felt like I was running out of gas.

I had walked through almost every water station, pouring water all over my head. I felt hot, and the sun did start to peak through the clouds. Mile 20 was a much-welcomed downhill and I started cruising again. Suddenly, everything felt good and I thought I could still PR, despite the bathroom break and the slowness of miles 14-19. But all of a sudden, I began to feel nauseated, and my stomach churned. I've been fortunate to never have an upset stomach during a race before. It happens to me a lot during long training runs, but never during races. So, I guess it was my day to finally join the ranks of the many runners who've had stomach issues during an actual race. I had to go to the bathroom really badly, and I started looking for places along the side of the road where I could go. I really didn't think I could wait for a porta potty, restaurant, or other official bathroom.

We ran through a residential area, and I asked someone standing outside of a house if he lived there. He said no and I said that I really needed a bathroom ASAP. He told me that there were some porta potties up to the left. It hurt so much to run, but I needed to get to those porta potties, or I was just going to explode! Finally, I made it to a porta potty at mile marker 22 and had a diarrhea attack. Ugh. It felt really good to finally go to the bathroom, but I realized how bad the situation had gotten.

The last four miles were awful. Even though I had gone to the bathroom, the pain moved to the right side of my belly button and felt like a cramp. Every time I ran, I felt a sharp pain, so I would walk. My stomach actually didn't hurt when I walked, but the moment I started running, it would cramp up. And as I expected, miles 20-26 were all downhill.

It was so frustrating. My legs felt good and I had plenty of energy. I didn't feel at all like I had hit "the wall," and yet my stomach was killing me. Other runners and cheerers encouraged me along, the way they do when someone is bonking. So even though I ran a smart race, and even though I wasn't *bonking, I still had that embarrassing I-am-walking-the-last-four-miles-of-this-marathon experience.*

I really wanted to drop out. But I didn't drop out because I was representing my company, a gold sponsor of the race. It would have reflected poorly on the company and I think I would have regretted it. The people I work with don't care how fast I finish, they only care that I do finish. If I had been doing this race just for myself, then I probably would have dropped out. But I was strong for my company and for St. Jude. Seeing the hospital and understanding the cause really helped power me through.

I finished in 4:14:38, which is my 3rd slowest out of 12 marathons. I also placed 57 of 188 in my age group, which is still respectable. As I finished, the medical people swarmed around me because they had seen me holding my stomach in pain. I assured them I was okay, and they backed off. I felt nauseated and tired, but I knew I would be fine once I sat down. I made my way up to my company's suite in the stadium where everyone was waiting for me. (I was the only one from our group who had run the full marathon. Everyone else had run the half—including Greg.) They were all very supportive and understanding. I was happy I finished and didn't bail out.

Even though I am in the best shape I've ever been in (well, maybe I was in better shape in the weeks leading up to NYC), I ran my third slowest marathon ever. I went into this race with no expectations and I ran it conservatively—based on feel—and I still had a bad experience.

I wonder when things are finally going to line up for me and when I'll be able to run a marathon that truly reflects all the training I've been doing. The last time I ran a good marathon was in March 2008—nearly three years ago. For over two years now, I've been consistently training harder and longer for my marathons, and my race times at other distances have dropped dramatically. My half marathon is down from 1:50 to 1:41, and my 5K is down from 23:30 to 22:21.

I feel wonderful about everything I've accomplished over the past three years, both in terms of my actual race times, and in terms of where I am mentally. I am much more relaxed about it now, although still as focused on training and racing to the best of my ability. So, I'm not really upset about this experience from yesterday. I'm not disheartened like I was after Bob Potts in May. I'm just wondering when I will get to run a marathon when I say, "Wow—I rocked it!" instead of "Oh, that was miserable."

I am going to continue training and doing what I love to do—run. My legs don't feel like I ran a marathon yesterday, because I didn't run a marathon. I walked most of the last four miles. I'm hoping to be back running by Tuesday.

PART III

A BREAKDOWN

CHAPTER 7:
FREE TIME

September 29, 2015

Today, the B.A.A. posted this message to their Facebook page:

*Due to the high level of interest in next year's race, we
unfortunately are unable to accept all entry applications received.
Those who submitted registration applications will receive an e-
mail detailing the status of their entry beginning tomorrow. The
B.A.A. also will announce what the "cut-off" time standard for
accepted registrants was this year. We at the B.A.A. are honored
by the interest shown by all seeking to run the Boston Marathon,
and thank all runners for their patience, support, and
understanding during the registration process.*

Tomorrow I will finally have official confirmation of my Boston
Marathon acceptance. It feels like I'm eight years old on Christmas
Eve, chomping at the bit to open all of my presents. Or even like
my teenage self—waiting eagerly at the mailbox for a college
acceptance letter. What will it feel like when I'm finally "in"?
After so much free time spent on training?

Free time. If I've learned anything throughout my journey,
I've learned that time is certainly not free. You have a limited
amount of time on this earth and how you choose to spend it says a

lot about who you are. According to my training log, I've spent 2,158 hours (or 89 days) of my life running since January 1, 2008. I've spent even more time—maybe three times that amount—thinking about my race times and training paces. *What pace do I need to run today to prove to myself that I am fast enough to qualify for Boston? What marathon time can I predict based on my race times at shorter distances?*

3 hours and 40 minutes. So much blood, sweat, and tears for 3 hours and 40 minutes. When I take a step back and look at how much of my life has been centered on marathon training, it's amazing to think that I did it all just to shave a few minutes off of my marathon time. And according to the B.A.A.'s Facebook post today, a 3:40 wouldn't have actually gotten me into the 2016 Boston Marathon.

* * *

I recovered from Memphis relatively quickly, and was ready to hit the ground running again by late December. I decided that even though I had a bad experience at the 2010 Shamrock Marathon, I would run it again the following March. If I qualified for Boston, it would mean running the 2012 race. However, I wasn't thinking about marathon running in terms of a BQ anymore. I basically just wanted to run my fastest possible race—a race that truly reflected my fitness level—and the byproduct of that would be Boston. As the new year kicked off, I put forth some goals.

January 2, 2011

I don't really have time-based goals for 2011. Although I would like to BQ and get my half marathon time under 1:40, my primary goal is to run a strong marathon. I'm not as focused on the time as I used to be. I have bonked in every single marathon I have run since March of 2008—that's going on three years of all bonks. My secondary goal is to increase my training mileage, ideally by an average of 5 miles a week, provided that I don't get injured. Of course, for most of these running goals to be achievable, staying injury-free is a must, so I guess that trumps the marathon goal.

I was fortunate to have run injury-free for all of 2010. I attributed that to running outside instead of on a treadmill. But when winter came and covered the ground in snow and ice, I was forced to return to the treadmill for many of my runs. Having not run on a treadmill since the previous April, my body wasn't used to it and I ended up with three stress fractures in my shins.

I began to feel some shin pain while running on the treadmill, and I immediately suspected that it might be a stress fracture. I remembered how depressed I became the last time I was injured and didn't want to go down that path emotionally. To keep my spirits high, I wrote a poem in my blog:

Woe is me.
I have an injury.
Few things are worse for a runner to face
I have to accept this will slow down my pace.
I am hopeful that it's just a shin splint
But it hurts when I walk, much more than a hint.
If this is a stress fracture I'm going to be mad
For the PRs I hoped for will not be had.

The only good thing I can think of to say,
I'd rather be injured now than in the month of May.
There's snow everywhere, so I'd be stuck on the 'mill
Just one long flat surface, not one single hill.
I think that's the culprit of my shin pain anyway,
Too much treadmill running, and now I'm having to pay.
Now it's pool running for me, and elliptical too
I cannot land run until the pain has been subdued.

I've been stretching and strengthening and treating with ice
Despite all these measures, my shin feels not nice.
Even at rest, I can feel a dull ache
I certainly hope my shin bone didn't break!
All of this makes me extremely frustrated,
I don't want my spring season to be so ill-fated.

My fitness had reached an exciting new peak,

Can I preserve it without 50 miles per week?
I did a 3-hour pool workout of running and swimming
And that seemed to be effective, and not at all skimping.

Woe is me.
I have an injury.
And what is the damage? That's left to be seen.

Even though it was only my right shin that hurt, the bone scan detected two stress fractures in the left leg (one on the tibia, one on the fibula) in addition to the one on my right tibia. The doctor's orders were simple: no running for six weeks. I could use the elliptical machine and the pool for cross training in the meantime.

I did everything in my power to accelerate the healing. One of my friends used a bone stimulator machine to shorten the healing time of a fracture in her foot. These machines had been shown to reduce healing time, so I purchased one off of eBay. (They retailed for $4000 and my insurance wouldn't have covered it unless it was a full break.) So the way to go, recommended by my friend, was to get one that had been gently used from eBay.

To maintain my fitness, I started deep-water pool running (with a flotation belt) with some swimming thrown in here and there. I had read quite a few articles and blogs on pool running, and there was a great deal of evidence that when done at the proper intensity, pool running could help you maintain most, if not all of your fitness over a six-week period.

Thankfully, there was a pool about two miles from my house. This meant that I could spend up to an hour and a half in the pool before having to leave for work. On the weekends, I started going to a pool about 30 minutes away to meet up with some friends. Even though I was injured, I still spent all of my "free time" on running-related activities. I tried my best to keep a positive attitude:

February 6, 2011

So far, this injury has not gotten me down as much as previous injuries. Mainly because I really think the pool running will preserve my fitness and there is nothing more disheartening than the belief that everything you've been working so hard for has gone to waste. Also, I just came off of a fantastic year of running, setting PRs at nearly every distance—except for the marathon, of course.

I was fortunate to be injury-free for 15 months, so I guess I was due. During that time I think I came a long way, and I can only hope for another long stretch of no injuries again once this is done with. Of course I am upset about this, but I am trying to focus on recovery, and not think about all the races I'm missing out on this season. The outpouring of support from my running friends has been incredible. Without them, I would know nothing of pool running and bone stimulators!

I'm determined to keep my spirits high and to preserve my fitness. I also need to be prepared to lose some of it. It will be such a letdown if the pool running doesn't work as well as expected, so I need to be cautiously optimistic.

* * *

Thankfully, the stress fractures only put a small dent in my running. The bone stimulator machine seemed to work well, and I was able to ease back into running after just four weeks instead of the typical six. The combination of pool running and the elliptical machine seemed to help maintain my fitness level, so I was still in decent shape when I returned to running.

Through pool running, I connected with a group of other runners, many of whom were members of Capital Area Runners, a local running club. I had known of this group for quite some time. They had a reputation for being fast runners and were easily identifiable at races with their bright red shirts.

I would have loved to have officially joined the Capital Area Runners, but the group runs took place in Arlington, which was a 30-minute drive from my house if there was no traffic. It didn't make sense to travel that far for a group workout, especially since my office was only five minutes away from my home. But it was nice to have met so many new friends through pool running.

Since running a spring marathon was out, I started to think about my next marathon. Greg and I ultimately settled on the Milwaukee Lakefront Marathon. It had everything that we were looking for. It was a medium-sized race with a great reputation, occurring early in the fall. The course profile was primarily flat with a few rolling hills.

March 9, 2011

The only drawback to Milwaukee is that I heard it could get windy in the last three miles near the lake. And that "Lakefront" is a misnomer because you don't even see the lake until the last few miles. And of course, with my luck, it could be really hot and spoil the whole thing for me, putting me on a nearly 4-year streak with no marathon PR, despite massive improvements at all other distances over the past few years. Yeah, I'm bitter.

Thinking about my marathon failures only upset me, so I tried as hard as possible to focus on my approach to safely resuming training. I had made significant strides when it came to mentally coping with injuries. My foot injury from 2009 had put me in a dark place, dominating my mental space for weeks. At the time, I had thought that nothing positive came from the foot injury, but ultimately it was a learning experience in tolerating time off from running.

When the stress fractures arrived in early 2011, I was determined not to travel down that same dark road. I was diligent about my pool running and swimming, and pool running even became a way for me to interact with other runners—most of whom were also injured in some way. Instead of focusing on the things I could not do, I focused on the things I *could* do to maintain my fitness. I focused on the process. The result? An unexpected PR in the 5K distance at the end of April.

CHAPTER 8:
RESTLESSNESS

One of the lingering side effects of my eating disorder was terminal insomnia—waking up earlier than needed with a feeling of restlessness. Initially, I would wake up at 3:30 or 4:00 with intense hunger pains. Over time, my body got used to waking up that early, and it was never a peaceful transition. The minute I awoke, I'd be ready to hop out of bed and go running. If I tried to lie in bed, I would feel anxious and nervous, as if I needed to be doing something. I hadn't felt relaxed or calm upon waking since my college days.

I had always expected that this would change if I ever got married. I thought that having someone to fall asleep with and wake up next to would make me "normal" again. But my sleep woes weren't something that a partner could cure—I had to figure it out on my own. And after years of living this way, it became my new normal. On the plus side, I never needed to set an alarm clock and I was very productive in the mornings. On the negative side, it severely limited my social life because I was so tired in the evenings. It was a restless, anxious existence, and my mind was never at peace.

* * *

In the spring of 2011, the B.A.A. announced that it was making its qualifying standards more difficult, due to increased demand for the race. They predicted that registration for the 2012 race would fill up immediately (which it did), and so for the 2013 race, they dropped all qualifying times by 5 minutes and 59 seconds. Instead of needing a 3:40:59 to qualify for Boston, I now needed to run a 3:35:00.

This drop in qualifying standards didn't faze me for several reasons:

1. I thought that I was capable of running a 3:35:00 or faster in Milwaukee.
2. Since the race was now even more difficult to qualify for, it became more prestigious, and therefore more desirable.
3. I would soon be turning 35, which meant that if I didn't get into the 2013 race with a 3:35:00 or faster, I could qualify for the 2014 race with a 3:40:00.

In July, I officially joined the Capital Area Runners (CAR). Because I had already made friends with so many of the women in the group, it seemed like it was worth the trek into Arlington once or twice a week to be a member. My first workout with CAR was hill repeats at the Iwo Jima Memorial. Led by Coach George, we ran up and down a long, gradually sloped hill six times. I enjoyed the camaraderie and team atmosphere. Plus, I had heard great things about Coach George, and I knew some runners who had improved significantly under his watch. Now that I had a coach, training looked a bit different for me.

July 9, 2011

I think that the longer training cycles, especially in the summer, wear me out too much, so I am cutting back to a 13-week program for Milwaukee. As for weekly mileage, it used to be standard for me to peak at around 60, and average in the upper 40's or lower 50's. But this time, I'm going to peak at around 55 and average in the mid 40's. I plan to supplement this with a pool running/swimming combo twice a week. I'd like to give myself one full rest day, so one of my pool days will be on the same day as one of my run days. So that's 4 days of running, 1 day of running +

pool, 1 day of pool only, and 1 rest day.

I used to do all my long runs in heart rate zone 2 (easy), with the exception of two of them, when I would throw some marathon pace miles in—sort of like the Pfitzinger approach. But George advocates breaking all the long runs up into thirds: the first third very easy, the second third moderately easy, and the last third at marathon pace to tempo pace. This isn't as challenging as it sounds if you start out slowly enough.

George asked me today what my goal for the marathon was, and I don't think I'll really be able to determine that until closer to the race. Right now I think that a 3:35 is realistic, and so does George, but I might adjust that faster or slower based on how training goes. And I didn't pick 3:35 because of Boston—that's simply the time that my training paces, heart rates and races suggest. I'm picking a goal based on what I think I can do, not based on the golden BQ standard that shaped my mindset for way too long and broke me down more times than I care to admit.

* * *

My Milwaukee Lakefront training cycle was nearly flawless. I felt like I was making great progress with CAR, and my two tune-up races were highly encouraging. I ran an 8K two weeks before the marathon in 35:53, which was an average pace of 7:13. This was faster than I expected, and according to the McMillan calculator, the equivalent marathon performance was 3:32:11.

Going into the marathon, it seemed like everything was finally coming together for me. The weather would be close to perfect and I knew I was in the best shape of my life. I tried my best to be confident and relaxed, but on a subconscious level, I was putting a great deal of pressure on myself. I had now been training to qualify for Boston for over three years. I had bonked in every marathon I attempted, and I wanted to run a strong marathon more than anything else in the world.

Finally I had my chance. This was it. I knew from experience that it took a lot for everything to come together on race day: no illness, no injury, and good weather. And here was my opportunity to finally, after three years, prove to myself and to the world that I was a "good" marathoner.

I didn't have a particular time goal in mind for this race. Coach George advised me to start at a pace of 8:20-8:30 for the first 10K, and then gradually speed up. I assumed he based his recommendation on my training paces and 8K tune-up race. He was a conservative coach with a firm belief in the "start slow, finish fast" approach, and based on my training runs, a starting pace of 8:25 seemed completely manageable.

October 2, 2011

My mentality going into the race was to "just do it" and let the race come to me. I know I tend to psych myself out over marathons, so this time was going to be different because I was going to relax and run by feel—like how I used to do before my series of failures.

During the first few miles I focused on being relaxed and enjoying the scenery. I listened to other people's conversations and was trying to focus on my surroundings instead of the fact that this was my marathon. It was a bit crowded and the 3:40 pace group was just ahead of me. I told myself that I shouldn't try passing them until after the 10K point, or even later if I didn't feel comfortable speeding up that soon.

It felt very easy. In fact, I could hear others around me breathing heavily. I knew I was in great shape because I felt like I wasn't exerting much effort at all. After mile marker 6 I knew I had the coach's OK to pick up the pace a bit, but I didn't feel quite ready for that. I knew I had a long way to go, and I wasn't ready to put on the gas just yet. I thought that maybe by mile 8, 9 or even 10 I would be ready to start picking it up. But instead, I began to feel worse and worse. Eight miles into the race, I knew something was wrong.

Yup, something was wrong. Once again, trying to stay mentally positive, I told myself it was okay if I couldn't speed up. I could just maintain this same pace, end up with a 3:40, and be happy with it. By mile 10 I knew my race was not going to end well. I felt exhausted and even a bit nauseous. I know that positive self-talk can go a long way, so I kept reminding myself that I was very well trained and that this feeling would pass. I would be able to maintain this pace for a while. I was doing great!

I crossed the halfway point at 1:50. I had planned on being there at around 1:48, so I wasn't too far off, but the fact that the race was no longer in my control at the halfway point was not a good sign.

Normally, hitting the wall is a sign of going out too fast—a rookie mistake. And if I had felt this tired at mile 19 or 20, then I would have thought that I went out too fast. But after only 8 miles at a pace of 8:27, I was already feeling "off," so I think that there must have been something else going on. After all, I recently ran 5 miles at a pace of 7:13 and felt fantastic at the end. During this race, I ran 8 miles at a pace of 8:27 and was feeling drained.

During the 15th mile, I went into a porta potty and then couldn't get going again. I realized that I didn't think I could run much farther. I still had 11 miles to go and I wanted to stop completely.

Then, the all-too-familiar "wall" things happened. I started getting passed by pace groups. The 3:45 group came and went, followed by the 3:50 group. It wasn't long before the 3:55 group showed up and passed me as well. I was reduced to a run-walk. I could only run for about 5 minutes at a time before feeling completely spent.

Greg had started the race behind me, and was planning to run at a 9:00 pace. I knew that eventually he would catch up to me, I just didn't know when. We had joked beforehand that he'd better not find me walking on the side of the course at mile 20, and that's exactly what did happen. He said his heart sank when he realized I was walking.

Having him at my side gave me a brief boost, and I was able to run with him for almost a mile until I had to stop again. I told him to finish and that I didn't want to ruin his race. He insisted on staying with me and I felt so guilty.

At this point, I sat down on the grass, and then laid down on the grass. I felt completely defeated. I could not go one step further. Greg stood over me with his arms extended, urging me to get up from the grass. I refused. I told him to continue on without me—I didn't want to ruin his race. Why should my own misery impact his experience? He reminded me that I wasn't injured and that I was perfectly capable of getting up from the grass. Even so, I resisted. I simply didn't have it in me to continue.

Greg refused to leave me there on the ground, and ultimately I forced myself to stand up again. The last five miles were torture. I started getting side stitches, and I felt like I needed to vomit. I was thirsty, but whenever I drank water, my stomach would revolt and I'd feel even more nauseated. I thought maybe I had overdone the hydration thing because my body wasn't able to handle any more water. I cried. I was devastated and I was hurting. I couldn't understand why this was happening to me again and why it always happened to me.

Maybe I drank too much water the day before and the morning of the race. I don't measure my water—I just try to drink lots of it along with electrolytes. Maybe I struck the wrong balance. Maybe I shouldn't have force fed myself so much food the day before because I had very little appetite. My best marathons were all run under cloudy skies—maybe I can't handle the sun at all.

I felt like I had ruined my husband's race and I had let everyone down. Why was this happening to me? Greg told me that I had the rest of my life to think about that, but for now I had to focus on finishing the marathon. I wanted to wallow and cry and not finish, but Greg helped me run/walk. We finished the race holding hands and I was so relieved to be done with it.

4:18:51. This was my third slowest marathon out of 13 and my 6th bonk.

I got my medal, but I wanted to throw it on the ground. I didn't feel like I deserved a medal and I didn't feel at all proud of myself. I didn't even want to take off my shoes (which is normally the very first thing I do post-marathon). I wanted to be miserable.

When we got back to our hotel I called my coach. I wanted answers and I knew he'd have them. He did. He said he had a feeling earlier in the week that this could happen to me, simply based on my Facebook wall. He said that the race got built up so much and that I had so many people tracking me that I likely caved under the pressure. He told me how he once won a half marathon in a time of 1:05 and was the favorite to win a subsequent marathon. But the pressure got to be too much and he ended up dropping out at mile 20. He said he's seen this happen before, when the athlete gets too hyped up about the race beforehand.

I was trying to NOT do this during my taper, but I couldn't help it. He told me I should have stayed away from Facebook the week before my race and relaxed more. Most importantly, he assured me that I was a good marathoner in great shape, and I should brush this one off and get there and try again as soon as possible.

I took what my coach said and then I combined it with what I knew to be true about my taper. Suddenly all the pieces started to fit. In the two weeks leading up to my marathon—the taper—I was a ball of anxiety. For those of us who love the adrenaline high of running, the taper is not a fun time. We're forced to cut back our mileage and simply rest up for the marathon. It sounds easy to non-runners: all you need to do is eat well, sleep well and relax. I know that these things are critical to marathon performance, but my anxiety often gets the better of me and this was my worst taper ever.

Aside from the usual taper anxiety, I was also dealing with other stresses. Squirrels were getting into my house, and Greg was out of town on business and unavailable to assist or help calm my nerves. Additionally, my job had been really stressing me out as the environment there is changing rapidly and we have a huge event coming up.

I was trying my best to not think about the race during my taper, but by doing that, I guess I made my physical anxiety worse. On a daily basis I dealt with:

- *Night sweats: waking up at around 2:00 a.m. covered in sweat*
- *Insomnia: Not being able to fall back to sleep after waking up at 2:00 a.m.*
- *Loss of appetite*

I lost 4 pounds in the two weeks before my race, and that's a lot for a person of my height. I could feel that my body was on overdrive, and I'd wake up in the middle of the night with my heart pounding. To combat all of this, I used Advil PM on some nights and was able to get a reasonable number of hours of sleep. The quality wasn't great, but I was sleeping so I thought I'd be fine for the race. Even though I wasn't at all hungry, I ate anyway.

Despite all of my anxiety and sleep issues, I never doubted that I would still have a great marathon—at least not consciously. I thought I had done everything right in terms of training, nutrition, hydration, etc. I went into the race with a good attitude and I didn't feel stressed on race morning. I had a healthy mindset during the race, but by that time it was too late.

I had already worn out my body in the weeks before my race with physical anxiety. This was my mistake, and this is where things went wrong. It's wonderful that I can identify what the problem was, but now I have no idea how to fix it. It's like when someone tells you not to think about an elephant, you can't help but think of an elephant. The more I tell myself to relax about the marathon and not to have anxiety during the taper, the more I will probably stress about it. And even if I shove it out of my mind, which I did during this taper, the anxiety is there under the surface.

I think I'm finally starting to see what has been going on with my previous marathons. The first 7 marathons I ran went perfectly and I exceeded my goal each time. The next 6 marathons were all bonks. Yes, some were weather related. But I think weather was only part of the problem.

Here's my theory. During my first 7 marathons, I didn't use a formal training plan and I ran relatively low weekly mileage. I was just doing my own thing and enjoying PR after PR. Physiologically, my V02 max test revealed that I work aerobically at a higher percentage of my max heart rate than most people, which means my body is more suited for distance than speed. I was a great marathoner. I always ran negative or even splits. It came naturally to me. 4:46, 4:24, 4:13, 4:05, 3:56, 3:51, and then a "fun run" in London of 4:11.

So I thought to myself, if I can run so well with no formal plan, just imagine what I could do if I followed a plan and increased the mileage! I could probably qualify for Boston! That's when I started following training plans with higher mileage. Along with this came huge PRs in other distances. My 2:00 half marathon PR gradually turned into a 1:41. My 53:00 10K shot down to a 46:34. Instead of a middle-of-the-pack runner, I was winning age group awards on a regular basis and was almost always in the top 5th percentile. And yet, the marathons started to go in the opposite direction. It was bonk after bonk after bonk, and I chalked it all up to being bad luck.

Yes, luck was a huge part of it, but the common factor in all of these marathons was ME. I was the problem. With every marathon bonk, the more and more determined I became not to bonk, the more and more anxiety would build up pre-race, and I couldn't perform. A good example of this is the Shamrock Marathon 2010. That was a very hot race. However, I started feeling awful at mile 10 before it even got to be 65 degrees. I quit at mile 13.5, and I felt like I had run a full marathon—I was so spent.

Another example is the Potomac River Marathon. That was my back-up race after my Shamrock disaster. However, when the extended forecast came out, calling for 70's and 90% humidity, I found another back-up two weeks later. I still went to the Potomac River Marathon with the intent of having it be a nice training run of 13 miles. But there was zero pressure on me because I wasn't racing it. As a result, I felt so great—despite the heat and humidity! I kept running and running—all the way to mile 18. Stupidly, I stopped because I wasn't on pace for a 3:40. I performed SO WELL at that race in horrible conditions because . . . I wasn't racing. I was relaxed.

The pieces of the puzzle are finally coming together for me and I know what the problem is. I know why I keep bonking. I have too much pre-race anxiety and it wears my body out. Unfortunately, this isn't something you can fix overnight like a hydration issue. I'm probably going to see a sports psychologist and really find a way to let go. I'll probably do another marathon later in the season, but I'm skeptical that I will be able to solve the anxiety issue before then. This has been snowballing for years.

The good news is that I do know how to run a great marathon. I've run seven of them that were well executed and perfectly paced without the help of the Garmin. I just have to find some way to get back there.

* * *

My Milwaukee experience left me heartbroken. It was all I could think about for days afterward, even though blog commenters and Coach George told me to simply "shrug it off." I looked into seeing a sports psychologist. One of my friends from CAR was seeing one, and she passed his name along to me. I contacted him and when I realized how expensive it was (and health insurance wouldn't cover it), I decided against it. It was a significant amount of money, and I knew exactly what I needed to work on. I told myself I would be committed to letting go of my anxiety and my obsessiveness around race times. Before seeking help from a professional, I figured I should try to do it on my own first and see where that got me.

October 12, 2011

I hate it when I meet someone new and I tell them I run marathons and then they ask me what my best time is. It's like they want to know how fast I am, and my marathon PR is how they are going to judge me—without knowing anything about my training or other races.

I know that I shouldn't care about what other people think, especially strangers I just met. But I think my marathon PR from 2008 is a misrepresentation of who I am as a runner, so I hate that question. I've come so far since then, and yet I still answer the "what's your fastest time" question the exact same way: the same 3:51 that it was in 2008.

It also annoys me when I hear about people who don't run much, and decide they want to run a marathon with the goal of qualifying for Boston. They run all their training runs at their goal pace, which goes against all of the expert approaches. They go into the marathon, qualify for Boston, and then move on to something else. And then there's someone like me, who should have been able to BQ over 3 years ago, who has read books about marathons, who has a coach, who wears a heart rate monitor, who wins age group awards at all other distances, and does everything "right," but then can't pull it all together on marathon day. It doesn't seem fair, but as we all know, life is not fair.

I know this is happening to me because I'm supposed to be learning something that is a lot larger than running. I need to work on being less anxious. I need to not be as perfectionistic. I have to be okay with the fact that many things are not within my control. I need to stop using numbers to validate my success. I need to be less uptight. These are all areas that I have tried to address in the past in which I've made significant progress. But apparently, I'm not where I need to be. These are the areas that I need to focus on—not my training or my marathon times.

Not focusing on a particular marathon time is exactly what I tried to do with Milwaukee. I actually didn't have a goal time, but rather a large range where I expected I would fall. I had a strategy about how I would run the race, and I was confident that my time would be good based on my fitness level.

I don't feel burnt out. I love running and I have never dreaded going into a run. If I could go run 10 miles right now, that would make me very happy! Even on days when my runs don't go well, I still enjoy them. Heck—I even enjoyed Milwaukee. It was a miserable experience, yes, but I enjoyed that I was there and that I was taking part in the event.

Running is "fun" for me, but I don't run for the sole purpose of fun. If fun were all I was after, I would find something else to spend my time on. I enjoy the challenge. I love the personal fulfillment I get out of each run. I love setting goals for myself and attaining them. While I'm far from burnt out, I'm definitely discouraged. I worked really hard all summer and now that the weather is finally nice, I am stuck in the pool recovering with no marathon glory and no idea how the rest of the racing season will play out.

CHAPTER 9:
SOUL SEARCHING

When you hit rock bottom it forces you to take a close look at yourself and how you got there. One of my favorite musicians, John Ondrasik, refers to this as "the devil at the bottom of the wishing well." My Boston Marathon wish threw me down a dark well, where I was forced to face my demons head-on before climbing out.

I've never been someone to shy away from introspection. As a child, my father often told me that I had "deep thoughts" and taught me the meaning of the word "introspection" before I was ten years old. I've always been willing and eager to learn more about myself, particularly if it meant there was an opportunity to improve. My mirror was too often distorted, though, which left me running in circles.

As I tried desperately to improve my attitude about marathon running, I didn't have a clear roadmap. Furthermore, I was impatient and would get frustrated at myself for not being able to fix all the problems I identified. Surely once I recognized that my own anxiety was sabotaging my races, I'd be able to get over it—or so I expected.

* * *

Despite my Milwaukee heartbreak, the rest of the fall racing season played out quite well. In many ways, I felt vindicated and validated that I had, in fact, made fitness gains with all of my training. I set two significant PRs in November. I ran the Veteran's Day 10K in DC and shattered my 46:34 PR by a minute and 15 seconds, down to 45:19. At a Thanksgiving turkey trot, I took that 22:18 from the spring all the way down to a 21:29, which was a huge breakthrough. It was my first ever race with an average pace of sub-7:00.

I was also getting ready for a major life change. After over six years of working for the same company, I decided to move on and I accepted a job offer from another company. I had stayed at that job for so long because I ran the entire marketing function. The company more than doubled in size while I was there, and I continually sought out new ways to grow and challenge myself. However, it was time for a change, so I moved to another software company.

This new company was much larger and sold educational software into public school districts, which seemed like a welcome change from manufacturing software. I wouldn't be running the entire marketing function, which was a conscious choice. I wanted to learn from someone more experienced than myself and see how things were managed at a large business. By making this move, I was stepping out of my comfort zone and choosing to tackle new challenges.

What did this mean for my running? I gave up a job that was located two miles from my house for one with an actual commute and longer hours. This meant that I would go back to waking up before 5:00 and running in the darkness. It was time to focus less on running and more on my career, and this new job was a great opportunity.

As for my next marathon attempt, I decided once again that I would return to the Shamrock Marathon in the spring. Even though I had a horrible experience there in 2010, I still loved that race and I was determined to experience the "high" that I did back in 2008.

* * *

As a new year kicked off, I came to the realization that I needed to put serious effort toward overcoming my anxiety issues. Anxiety was the culprit. Anxiety was the reason I couldn't perform to the best of my physical ability. It didn't matter how fit I was—I would simply not be able to run a marathon in such an anxious state of mind. Now that I had identified the problem, I could begin to find a solution. I started blogging more about my attitude and mentality and less about the details of my training.

February 12, 2012

It's very tempting to write a post that recaps my training over the past few weeks, complete with split times and mileage totals, but I'm going to tackle a different subject matter.

I've had many, many successful training cycles. Suffice it to say, I'm good at training! I'm very consistent and dedicated to running and I have been since day one. In the past four years, none of those training cycles resulted in a good marathon. None of them. So I'm not going to address my progress with this cycle (at least not in this post), because it's not the kind of progress that I really need at this point.

I need a healthier mindset. I've been working on this for about two years now, but change doesn't happen overnight, so I'm still working on it. What do I mean by "healthier mindset?" When I met my husband back in 2009, my attitude about running was as such:

- *I followed a training plan to the letter and was disappointed with myself if I didn't make my weekly mileage goal.*
- *I didn't listen to my body and would do all runs as scheduled, even if I was tired or I felt an injury coming on.*
- *I was focused on time as the only indication of a good run or race, disregarding how the run felt.*
- *I was competitive with others and frustrated when I saw other people get faster at running while I wasn't progressing as much.*
- *Everything in my life revolved around my running. It was my top priority.*

- *I needed to prove to others that I was fast.*
- *I had to qualify for the Boston Marathon because that was the ultimate determination of whether or not I was a fast marathoner.*

Doesn't sound like much fun, does it??? A lot of this stuff is deep within my personality, and I don't intend to change who I am at my core. I will always be competitive, dedicated, and self-critical. I will always care about how others perceive me. But the extent to which I allow these elements of my personality to overtake my mindset and ultimately wreak havoc on my marathons can certainly be reduced.

* * *

March 4, 2012

I've been doing some self-therapy and self-exploring lately. As I continue on my journey to transition from super-obsessive, stressed-out runner to a calmer overall mental state, I've been thinking about where time fits in.

To start, I began thinking about what my marathon time used to mean to me. I had to get a 3:40 or less. I had to! I knew that an 8:25 average pace would get me a 3:40:59 and an 8:23 would get me a 3:40:00, and I thought about these numbers constantly. I fantasized about crossing the finish line and seeing those numbers on the clock.

And—I felt entitled. I felt like I had done the training, I was in good shape, and therefore I deserved a specific time. If something went wrong on race day, then I would feel like a huge injustice was done to me. After the Bob Potts Marathon in May of 2010, when I ran a disappointing 3:53, I started to realize how unhealthy this obsession with time was. I was tired of putting so much stock in a marathon time. It was making me feel awful.

Next up was the NYC Marathon, which I ran for fun with my husband, followed by the Memphis Marathon four weeks later, which wasn't a target race. It wasn't until the fall of 2011 that I gave the marathon another serious try. Knowing how unhealthy my time-based thoughts were, and being a black-and-white thinker, I went in the complete opposite direction: "Time doesn't matter at all," I thought to myself. "This is about enjoying the race and having fun. I don't have a time goal. I don't care about my time. I'm not stressed! I'm totally cool."

Lies, of course. And they will always be lies. Deep down, I didn't truly buy into that, and so I stressed about the race, didn't sleep well, and ended up bonking shortly after the halfway point. Once again, I was making rules for myself about how stressed I was allowed to be. Rules about how I couldn't focus on pace or time. I definitely had made progress from 2010, but the absolutes were still there. I was lying to myself, which made it even harder because I had to deny that my time mattered at all.

This left me wondering, so now what? I don't want to be obsessive about a time goal, but I don't want to lie to myself and say it doesn't matter. I started to think about why it did matter so much to me for so long. For years, I would often ask myself why I cared so much about getting a specific time. And the answer was always, "I just do!" When I really thought about it, I saw my marathon time as the validation of all my hard work—"proof" that I was as fast and as capable a runner as I believed myself to be. But at the same time, I knew I was working hard, so why the need for validation?

Looking back, I think it was insecurity. I needed that marathon time to prove to myself that I was capable. I also needed for everyone else to know that I was capable. I used to do the same thing with my weight. I needed the scale to read out a particular number to validate that I was thin—that I was "good" at being in control of my eating. And of course that's not a healthy attitude!

Back to my original question: what does time mean to me now? And what do I think it should mean to me? The second question is easier. I do consider myself an athlete and I am a competitive person by nature. I don't want to change who I am, so I think time should matter to some extent. I think I should set my sights on some kind of target range (as opposed to an exact time) and then on race day, focus more on the strategy/execution than on that ultimate goal.

What does it mean to me now? And do I have a goal for my

marathon in two weeks? I don't really know what time means to me now. I'm still thinking about that one. Maybe the answer is simply "it doesn't mean as much as before." I don't think I need it to validate that I've been working hard. I've had some fantastic workouts so I know that my fitness is solid. I haven't given much thought to my marathon time during this whole cycle, so I guess that's a step in the right direction. I also realized that I don't know how the paces line up with the times. I haven't spent any time on the pace calculator trying to correlate specific paces with finish times. Now that they've lowered the BQ standard, I actually don't know the specific pace of a BQ.

Why haven't I looked? Because it doesn't really matter based on what I am trying to do time-wise. I think I can run an average pace of anywhere from 8:00-8:20, so I'll start slower than 8:20, run conservatively the first half and then see how I feel. My coach has a pace chart for workouts and I have been using the 3:30 paces as a guideline. I've always been able to hit these paces, but at the same time, I don't expect a 20+ minute PR.

Regarding PRs, it's been four years since I've run a good marathon (although I technically set a 40-second PR in May 2009). I do believe that everything happens for a reason, so I have let go of my anger around this. I think the purpose here is that I am being pushed to become mentally healthier. Just like I had to experience so many relationship failures in order to work on myself, and ultimately meet my wonderful husband. I need to make my marathon time less of a priority and my relationship with myself more of a priority.

I am fully aware that anything can happen on race day, and I am prepared for whatever the day may bring. I just want to be okay. No matter what time I get, I want to be able to fall asleep the night after my marathon at peace with myself.

PART IV

A REVELATION

CHAPTER 10:
A SELF-FULFILLING PROPHECY

I'm firm believer in the concept of a self-fulfilling prophecy. Think of your worst fear, obsessively take actions to prevent it from happening, and it's more likely to come true. For example, if your biggest fear is getting into a car accident, you may be an overly cautious driver, driving in ways that others on the road might not anticipate. Slamming on the brakes when there's no real danger of bumping into something, driving well below the speed limit, or unnecessarily stopping could ultimately result in a crash, even though the intent of those behaviors was to prevent an accident.

My worst fear was hitting the wall in the marathon, and it was amplified by warmer-than-expected weather. While it is physiologically more challenging to run in warmer temperatures, it doesn't necessarily translate into hitting the wall. In my case, my experience was a double-edged sword. On one hand, experience had taught me that I didn't tolerate heat well, so I needed to slow down and take a more conservative approach. On the other hand, I had never run a satisfying race in the heat, so I expected all warm races to be miserable.

One of my self-fulfilling prophecies was that warm weather would lead to failure. It was anchored in reality, but my intense hatred of the heat set me up for failure before I even began the race. A more balanced approach would have been to simply focus on running to the best of my ability in the heat—whatever the outcome may have been. Running in the heat is its own unique challenge, and instead of embracing it, I cowered from it.

My other self-fulfilling prophecy was that anxiety and lack of sleep would cause me to run a "bad" marathon. Once I discovered that anxiety was the root of my problem, I tried desperately to reduce it. The more I tried to reduce it, the more intense it became. I was at war with myself—I was turning my greatest fears into realities.

* * *

Despite desperately trying to let go of my race anxiety and my perfectionistic attitude about marathoning, Shamrock was a bust. It was unseasonably warm, *again,* but in the spirit of letting go of my anxiety, I tried to ignore the weather. Despite my best efforts, however, I could not shake the memories of Shamrock 2010, when I had to drop out of the race due to heat exhaustion. Heat was the enemy, plain and simple.

I knew that agonizing over the weather would only cause me undue stress, so I told myself that the weather didn't matter. I was determined to not let the weather affect my race, come hell or high water!

Even with a conservative start, things started to get hard for me by the 8th mile. By mile 11, I was running a 9:00 pace and it felt like a 7:30 effort. By mile 12, I wanted to stop. I got to the halfway point having averaged a pace of 8:38, and then pulled off the course because I didn't feel like I could continue running.

I felt so defeated by the experience that I didn't even write an in-depth race report like I always had. Instead, I wrote a post titled, "Same Shit, Different Day."

March 19, 2012

I'm going to save myself some time here and ask you to read my 2010 Shamrock Race Report for a summary of what went on during yesterday's race. Click on this link, read the report, and then come back.

And there you have my 2012 Shamrock Marathon race

report! Too sunny, not acclimated, felt tired at mile 9, wanted to stop at mile 11, pulled off the course halfway. And just like in 2010, those 13.1 miles took a lot out of my legs, even though my average pace was the equivalent of my "easy" long run pace (8:38).

I'm through with analyzing why this happens to me over and over and over. Sleep, hydration, being relaxed, starting slowly, not obsessing over my goal time—I've addressed all of these issues. My coach tells me I need to figure out what I am doing differently on race day, but I don't have any answers. It is what it is.

I want to quit running marathons, but both my coach and my husband tell me that I need to keep at it—that one day it will all come together for me. One day, my 4-year streak of bonks and DNFs will come to an end. I don't know if I believe them, but I really enjoy training for marathons so I guess I'll keep doing it. I used to be a good marathoner. But that was over four years ago and maybe I just don't have it in me anymore.

I don't have much else to say about this. Same shit, different day.

This post received an outpouring of support from my blog followers and friends. Everyone wanted to help me, and some people offered suggestions, but I still felt completely defeated. I received quite a few comments with varying perspectives:

"Sometimes the answers to these issues are within us. It's just that we're blind to them and need to work hard and honestly to figure them out."

"It's honestly NOT your physical ability ... have you ever thought about looking into a sports psychologist? Maybe it's a true race mental block you have to work through."

"While I don't think giving up is ever the right option, I do think you might benefit from focusing on some shorter distance races for a while to build back your confidence. No use in beating a dead horse if you are afraid of experiencing another type of letdown."

"Don't dwell on negative experiences. The marathon relies on all things coming together perfectly during race day and in such a long race, that is A LOT of things."

I took a few days to recover mentally and reflect on all the comments and everything that happened. I came back to the blog a few days later.

March 21, 2012

I've gotten a lot of feedback on my Shamrock experience, and since my recap was rather grim, I feel the need to address some of the comments. I'm not feeling much better about the situation, but I am going to continue running and training and doing what I love to do. I'm upset about this and I am going to allow myself to be upset until time makes it all better. Most of the comments fell into three buckets:

1. Figure out what you do differently on marathon day so that you can address the issue and run great marathons. *My coach is in this camp. My response is that I'm fresh out of ideas. I don't do anything differently on race day. Really the only difference is that I hydrate more, but I get plenty of electrolytes too, so I don't think I am over-hydrating. I have the same shoes, the same nutrition, the same fitness level, the same sleep. I can't pinpoint anything, which is why I think there could be a subconscious mental aspect.*

2. You had a bad day—don't over-analyze it. Just get back out there. *I could have said this in 2010. But it's happened so many times that there has to be something going on.*

3. Focus on shorter distances (aka don't run marathons). *Shorter distances are great and I focus on them quite a bit. But I will continue to believe in myself and in my ability to run a great marathon. I have done it many times before and I will be able to do it again.*

I don't have any real solutions. I think that the next time I run a marathon, I'm not going to try to relax. I'm not going to try to "work" on my attitude. I am just going to be me. I am going to let myself feel whatever I feel—anxiety, excitement, fear, longing— I'm just going to go with it. And I'm going to wear headphones next time. Somewhere along the way I told myself that it wasn't good to wear headphones during a marathon. Maybe I need some music to get me outside of my own head and pull me along. I don't train with headphones because I am usually running with others. But when I run alone, I have music and I like it. Time to get some sleep.

* * *

I decided to go under the radar with my next marathon. I didn't blog about it beforehand. I didn't post about it on Facebook or Twitter. I didn't even tell my Capital Area Runners friends, except for one person. I had become fairly close with a woman named Amy. Amy and I had a fair bit in common. We both kept blogs, we both trained with CAR, and we both had had several recent marathon disappointments. In fact, when I DNFed at Shamrock, she was the first person I called when I got my cell phone from the baggage check area for support.

Amy was also trying to qualify for Boston and like me, made an attempt in the early spring that didn't get her there. Without even knowing that she had signed up for the Potomac River Marathon, I signed up myself. This was the same race that I had run back in 2010 as a training run, and had stopped at mile 18. It was a low-key, local event and I was familiar with the course. Amy and I even did a training run on the course prior to the marathon.

I decided to wear my heart rate monitor during this race. Typically, I only wore it during training, but I decided I would wear it for this marathon and keep my heart rate in the easy zone. During training, I could keep my heart rate in the easy zone and average a pace of 8:25 for about an hour. I determined that if I was truly going to figure out my marathon problem, I needed this heart rate data. My only goal was to have a strong finish, even if the time was slow. I intended to run the race at my easy pace just like I did in 2010 to see what would happen.

I titled my race report "Science Project."

May 6, 2012

I conducted a little science project today. I attempted to run the Potomac River Marathon with the goal of simply finishing strong—no matter how slow. I ran this race in 2010 as a training run, and I am in much better shape now than I was back then. Today's weather was cooler, so one might expect that with better fitness and cooler conditions, I would perform better. But that was not the case.

In case you didn't guess, I did not finish today's marathon. Really, what would the point be? I wasn't going to finish strong. I felt like death at a pace of 9:45. Three weeks ago, I ran a 21-miler at an average 8:58 pace in much warmer, sunnier weather. And my legs felt fine the next day—no lingering soreness.

What I'm getting at here is that this is a very physical manifestation of something 100% mental. Mention the word "marathon," and something happens in my brain and subsequently my body that makes me incapable of even running at my easy training pace. It's not lack of sleep. It's not dehydration. It's not the weather. It's not my fitness level. It's not over-training. It's not nutrition. It's not going out too fast. It's in my head and whatever "it" is, I can't get it out.

It's not as easy as just trying to relax. The more I try that, the worse it seems to be. In fact, today I was in high spirits, completely in it to have a good race. Time wasn't even an element here. I wasn't focused on time, and I wasn't obsessively looking at my Garmin. I listened to my music and treated it like a long run. But it didn't work.

When I stopped at mile 18.5, I watched the runners go by. Almost everyone was looking strong. I felt like death. I couldn't even communicate properly when I first stopped. Why me? Why can't I just be normal like everyone else? Why do I have to have this flipping complex about the marathon?

I won't stop running them. I'm not a quitter and I won't give up. I will figure it out. Maybe not in time for Richmond this fall. Maybe not in time for a spring marathon next year. But eventually, one day, it will happen for me.

* * *

I found myself in a deep depression after my experience at the Potomac River Marathon. It was as if a dark cloud was hanging over my head all day and all night, and I couldn't shake it off. Greg had never seen me so depressed. This was even worse than when I injured my foot back in 2009. I felt helpless. I had tried *everything* I could possibly think of to run a strong marathon, and I kept failing.

Amy qualified for Boston during the Potomac River Marathon. I watched her finish, as she seemed to glide effortlessly across the finish line with a PR and BQ in hand.

"Congratulations!" I exclaimed, trying my best to forget about my own misery.

"Thanks," she said, with a smile on her face. "What happened with you?" she asked.

"I have no idea," I said honestly. "I just felt horrible. I wasn't able to finish."

"It's in your head, " she replied, without further elaboration. I wanted to ask her what she meant by that. I was desperately seeking some words of wisdom or consolation that would somehow make me feel better. But I didn't want to bring her down and ruin her special moment, so I didn't have an extensive conversation with her about my issues. She was obviously excited about her performance and as we said goodbye, she repeated to me that it was "in my head."

I took her words to heart. Yes, I knew the problem was my anxiety, but I tried to address that and it didn't work. In fact, it kept getting worse and worse with each marathon.

CHAPTER 11:
RELIEF

September 30, 2015

At 11:27 a.m., I sit in a conference room at work, alone. I check the Boston marathon entrant database and my name pops up. A few minutes later, an email appears in my inbox:

Dear Elizabeth Clor,
*This is to notify you that **your entry** into the 120th Boston Marathon on Monday, April 18, 2016 **has been accepted**, provided that the information you submitted is accurate.*

I look at the email, and I have no immediate emotional reaction. The wait is over. I'm in. I take a few moments for myself. I expect to feel a huge sense of relief now that I am officially confirmed to run the Boston Marathon. But instead, I realize that I've felt "relieved" ever since I learned to let go of the obsession. Receiving this acceptance email is not some miraculous moment in time for me—it's simply another step in the journey. I'm happy. I'm content. I smile to myself as I exit the conference room and continue on with my workday.

* * *

Shortly after the Potomac River Marathon, I decided it was time to give the sports psychologist a try. Yes, it was a large investment in time and money, but I had gotten to the point where I didn't feel mentally healthy. My primary objective for seeking professional help was to not feel so horrible about my life and myself every time a marathon didn't go well. I needed a healthier mindset about running because my unhealthy mindset was impacting every aspect of my life. Ultimately, I wanted to be able to rid myself of my race anxiety and perform well at marathons, but that was just part of what I hoped to gain. I wanted to be at peace with myself first and foremost. The depression was simply not sustainable.

I contacted the sports psychologist and we agreed that I would see him on a weekly basis. His name was Neal Bowes, and his office was a 25-minute drive from where I worked. I secured a regular evening time slot with him each week, lasting one hour. Aside from coming highly recommended to me by another runner, his credentials were impressive. He worked with Olympic and elite athletes across a wide range of sports and taught at George Washington University. I knew that if I were going to address my issues, then I would have to trust him 100 percent.

During my first visit, I recounted the long saga of my failed BQ attempts over the years, and my recent anxiety-induced DNFs. I also gave him an overview of my eating disorder and how I recovered from that when I started running marathons. Hearing it out loud made me wonder why I didn't start seeing a sports psychologist sooner. I had spent the past four years of my life tortured by not being able to attain one simple goal. Why did it have to be so hard?

"You're absolutely correct, it is simple," said Neal. "Running is a simple sport. Many people over-complicate it and that's where problems often come in." Neal's sports psychology practice was actually named Simply Performance Group (SPG) because his philosophy was based on the notion that performing well is simple.

Upon listening to my story, Neal was able to boil my struggles down to a single issue: perfectionism. "At your core, you are a perfectionist," he told me. "Perfectionism is central to how you live your life and how you think about things. The good news is that perfectionism can be useful when you know how and when to apply it. I call that 'adaptive perfectionism,' and that's what I will work on with you. That said—we're not going to tackle perfectionism head-on right away. First, we're going to start chipping away at the edges so that we do this in manageable chunks."

I walked out of that appointment feeling relieved. I knew I had a long way to go, but at least I had some direction. I knew I was on the right path, and I was determined to devote myself to overcoming my issues. If I could overhaul my entire mindset and become an "adaptive perfectionist," then that achievement would far surpass any marathon goal.

* * *

"Are you a runner?" Neal asked me a few weeks later.

"Yes," I replied.

"No," he corrected me. "You are a person. Running is something you *do*." Neal drew a circle on his whiteboard. "At the center of this circle is who you are." He drew a dot at the center. "Your core values, your beliefs, and your personality traits are central to who you are. Running," he said as he drew a dot on the circumference, "is not who you are, it's something you do. Don't define yourself by the things that you do."

Neal called this concept "separation"—the ability to separate myself as a person from my running. This concept wasn't entirely new to me. I had known for years that using my race results to measure my self-worth wasn't healthy, and so I tried not to do it. It was similar to my eating disorder, when my entire identity became wrapped up in how much I weighed. Despite this self-awareness, I had made little progress in this area, and I could never shake the feeling that I wasn't "good enough" until I qualified for Boston.

We discussed this topic at length, and he asked me to think about ways in which I could view myself that had nothing to do with running or the "things I did." What were my core values? What were my beliefs? What type of person was I? Defining my core self wasn't about the things I did and the goals that I accomplished—it was about *how* I accomplished them.

"Can you just say 'I'm a good person doing good things?'" he questioned.

At that moment, I struggled to hold back the tears. Something about that statement saddened me greatly. I didn't respond. "A good person doing things" was not at all how I thought about myself or how I wanted to think about myself. My translation of that statement was "I'm ordinary." And ordinary was the worst thing I could possibly be. I needed to be far better than good. I needed to be excellent. Fantastic. Far above average. Not "a good person doing good things." Was Neal telling me that I needed to accept that I was just plain old ordinary? I couldn't do that.

On the drive home I let everything sink in. *A good person doing good things.* I thought about that over and over again. No, that wasn't at all how I saw myself. I saw myself a highly motivated person who was passionate about many things—my job, my piano playing, my blog, my husband, and of course my running. I didn't do things halfway—I went all-in on whatever I decided to commit myself to. *A good person doing things. Anyone can be a good person doing good things. That's so ordinary.*

I felt like Neal was asking me to give up on something core to my being—my passion and drive to accomplish great things in life. I equated "good" with "mediocre," and it's not where I wanted to be. Even still, I trusted Neal and I had faith that ultimately everything would work out the way it was meant to.

* * *

I had a love/hate relationship with the Lawyers Have Heart 10K. It was my first major road race in 2005 and I had run it every year since. I loved that I had a streak going and this race was always exciting for me. On the other hand, I hated how hot the race was. The race was always held in early June, which meant that it was hot, but I wasn't yet acclimated.

When I ran this race in 2006, my time was slower than it had been in 2005. It was my first disappointment since I had started racing, and I was surprised at how badly it made me feel. I was depressed about it for several days afterward. I kept thinking that I had run so much more in the past year than any other year, and yet I was somehow slower.

Now that I was working with Neal, I used this 10K as an opportunity to use some of the so-called "tools" he was equipping me with. One of these tools was the post-race review. The post-race review was a structured approach to assessing my performance in an objective manner. The goal was to identify the aspects of the race that went well and celebrate those, but also to learn from the experience. Neal asked me to set aside time shortly after each race to review it, and once I was done with the review, he advised me to move on with the rest of my day.

"It may sound clinical," Neal said, "but give yourself specified times when you think about running. Do not allow running to continually overtake your thoughts throughout the day. Set some boundaries within your brain. It will be difficult at first, which is why you need to be structured about how and when you think about your races."

Because I was accustomed to writing race reports in my blog, I simply added the structured review to the end of my 10K report.

June 9, 2012

One of the things I am working on with my new sports psychologist is the post-race "review." We've identified that I am very black and white in my thinking, and that unless I amaze myself with my performance, then I'm devastated. There isn't any middle ground. So for practice, here are some of the things that I automatically felt once the race was over and I heard that some of my CAR friends had set PRs.

- *I ran two minutes slower than my PR. Nobody else was that far off.*
- *Could the heat really have impacted me more than everyone else? No. I just wimped out. I didn't push as hard as I could have.*
- *47:18. It sure would have been nice to get into the 46's.*
- *It was a mistake to start off so slowly. I should have had more confidence than that.*

I know these feelings and thoughts don't get me anywhere. They are counterproductive and they don't build confidence. They serve no purpose and I am being unreasonably hard on myself. The post-race review is designed to replace these negative thoughts with a more objective analysis:

50% of the review: What went well?
- *I had a strategy*
- *I executed the strategy exactly as planned*
- *I beat my course PR by over two minutes*
- *I ran negative splits and didn't blow up—which was one of the key goals*
- *I was in the top 5% of my age group, and this is a competitive race*
- *I kept a positive mindset while running the race*
- *I had a really nice final kick, passing most people*
- *I enjoyed it (as much as one can enjoy the pain of a 10K!)*
- *I ran the tangents*

30% of the review: What Worked? What didn't quite work?
- *Worked: My nutrition and hydration*
- *Worked: Focusing on my form worked*
- *Worked: Keeping a positive attitude during the race worked*
- *Didn't quite work: not having a ballpark goal*
- *Didn't quite work: being intimidated by my past performances in this race*
- *Didn't quite work: not asking myself if I could push harder during the race*

20% of the review: What should I adjust for next time?
- *Have a ballpark time goal, and know an approximate pace I want to run—adjust that if necessary during the run*
- *Don't let past performances affect my confidence for future ones*

Now the key is to not view this as a "bad performance" and to not let it feed negativity into other races. There were a lot of positive things that came out of today's race—particularly in the area of strategy and execution. And a new course PR! I am just a bit disappointed in my finish time and the fact that I let this race intimidate me. There are some good things to learn from here.

Finally, an important point that my sports psych makes is that once the review is over, move onto something else. Do not dwell on it all day.

Neal asked me to apply this same methodology for each workout and each week of training. With a structured review process, I would end up with a more objective and useful assessment of my performance, rather than a purely emotional one. Plus, the quicker I was able to move past a disappointment, the better. The longer it festered, the more likely it would be to impact my mindset for future workouts and races.

Even if a workout or a race went really well, I shouldn't bask in that for too long either. It all came back to the concept of separation. *I am not a runner—I am a person who runs.* If I was constantly thinking about running, then I was allowing it to occupy too much headspace.

* * *

A few weeks after the 10K, I came down with a wicked sore throat. At first, I thought it was strep, but I tested negatively for that. It got worse and worse over the next few days, and I was so exhausted I could barely move. I turns out that I had mono.

I didn't realize it was mono at first. It was only after having been sick for so long that I was finally diagnosed with it. Once the initial sickness passed, my primary symptoms were weakness, fatigue, dizziness, and muscle aches. The illness had its ups and downs, and there were times that I was actually able to go to work and go see Neal. There were even times when I attempted running, but it never went well.

Every time that I thought I was on the mend, I'd push it by trying to run or going to work, and then I would just feel miserable the following day. Ultimately, I decided I needed to get serious about making a full recovery, so I didn't leave the house for several weeks—I just rested. Thankfully, the company I worked for was flexible, and I was able to work from home. I was extremely fortunate that Greg never caught my illness and he took care of me the entire time.

I came to terms with the realization that running a fall marathon was out of the question, but I was hopeful I would be able to run a half marathon by mid-November. Greg and I had both registered for the Richmond Marathon, which occurred later in the fall racing season, so I simply switched my registration to the half marathon.

Emotionally, I stayed relatively strong throughout the whole ordeal. I actually thought that the timing of the illness coincided perfectly with my primary goal of working through my running issues. It allowed me to truly take a step back from running, gain some perspective, and spend time thinking about all of the concepts Neal was teaching me. Even though I was weak and simply walking around the house felt exhausting, I knew I would ultimately get better and that this was the time for mental training instead of physical training.

Of course I had heard stories of Chronic Fatigue Syndrome, and part of me was worried that I would never be the same after this illness. The longer I remained sick, the more worried I became that I would forever struggle with this virus. I tried not to think about that, though, and I remained positive for most of the time that I was ill.

The Summer Olympics was in full swing, and as I watched the various events on TV, I looked at the athletes through an entirely new lens. I had always thought that to be really good at something, you needed to be 100% focused on it, to the point of obsession. But it turned out this was not the case. I wrote a blog post about my observations.

August 12, 2012

5 Things I Learned From the Olympics

One of the few upsides of having mono is the opportunity to watch plenty of the Olympic events. I've never been as engaged in the

Olympics as I have been this year, and I've made some interesting observations. I've been working with a sports psychologist, and these athletes have demonstrated many of the things I'm learning from him. I doubt I would have picked up on any of these things without his guidance. But the fact that I did pick up on them shows that I am really beginning to evolve my thinking and attitude about my own running.

1. Don't compare yourself to others. *I would assume that all athletes are competitive by nature, so how do you not compare yourself to others? How do you stay focused on your own performance, your own training, and your own goals when the sport is, by nature, competitive? Surely once you get to the Olympic level you are comparing yourself to others constantly, right? Wrong.*

I was watching the men's synchronized diving, and there was an interview with one of the divers shortly after his dive. (I think it was Troy Dumais.) He said that usually once he finishes his dive, he doesn't watch the other people dive or watch for their scores—he just waits to see how things play out. He was focused on his own performance and not at all concerned with the other divers in the competition. I thought to myself, "What a healthy approach! If that were me, I would probably have my eyes glued to those diving boards and the divers' scores."

2. Focus on the race itself, not a time goal. *More generally speaking, focus on the process, not the outcome. One of the things I have been trying to overcome for years is focusing too much on my time goals. I've tried to NOT think about my time goals, but my sports psychologist says that that approach is just avoidance. What I really needed was something else to focus on. Telling yourself to NOT think about something without having an alternative TO think about doesn't work. Neal told me to focus on the "process" of the race, and the aspects of the race that were in my control.*

After one of the track semi-finals, a reporter was interviewing one of the runners. She said that his times were close enough to potentially beat the world record and was that something he was aiming for in the finals? His response was that he was not focused on beating the world record, but just to run the best race that he could. (I forget who this was and if he did actually beat the world record, but regardless, he's very much on target with being focused on the process, not the outcome.)

3. Your sport is not who you are. It's something you do. *It's plastered all over running magazines and Facebook walls: I AM A RUNNER! According to my sports psychologist, it's a much healthier attitude if your sport is not who you are, but rather something that you do. Separation. You cannot let your sport consume you and determine your mood 24 hours of the day. You focus on running when it's time to run or to work on a training plan. Otherwise, you should be focused on whatever else you are doing—working, spending time with the family, relaxing, getting together with friends. If you're at that level, how can it not consume your whole life? I mean, what else is there if you are training 10 hours a day and are at the top of your sport!?*

I saw some interviews with Katie Ledecky's friends in Bethesda, MD. For those of you who haven't been following the Olympics, Katie is a 15-year-old who won gold in the 800m freestyle. Her friends all said pretty much the same thing about her: "If you were talking to her, you wouldn't even know she was a swimmer. She's really down to earth and modest about it." It sounds like that when Katie is socializing with friends, she's focused on her friends and not telling them all about her swimming. I would guess she's done a great job at keeping her swimming life in the pool and other elements of her life separate.

4. If you look for failure, you will be sure to find it. *Very similar to "you can't please everyone all of the time." For some reason, people are so quick to judge these Olympic athletes. As a perfectionist, I hate the idea of anyone thinking that I did something wrong or that I failed at something. But the reality is that we can't control other people, and there will always be critics.*

Gabby Douglas won the individual all-around gymnastics gold medal. And yet many people were criticizing her hair. I was shocked to learn this because a) who cares about her hair—she's fantastic! And b) what's wrong with her hair? It's pulled back like everyone else's! Even if you win a gold medal at the Olympics, there will still be critics. External critics are a fact of life, we can't control them. But we can make sure that we aren't our own internal critics.

5. Performance is dynamic. You aren't a machine. *One of my greatest frustrations as a runner (and I'm guessing most runners share this frustration) is when you run a race significantly slower than what you know you are capable of. You have an off day. I tend to really beat myself up when this happens, but my sports psychologist is constantly reminding me that performance is dynamic, I'm not a robot, and there are no guarantees that I will be able to perform at my peak on race day. In fact, he said that among the world's top marathoners, most of them say that only 1 out of every 5 marathons is a good race for them. Bottom line— you cannot expect peak performance at every race, and sometimes it's just not there. Often, the only explanation for a sub-par performance is that some days are simply better than others.*

Gymnast McKayla Maroney performed a near perfect vault in the team competition and was expected to easily win gold in the individual vault competition. But she fell on her butt—something that she had never done at a competition before. Does this mean McKayla suddenly became any less of a gymnast? Did her abilities disappear overnight? No. She just had an off day, and it's normal for something like that to happen. Of course the poor girl was a target for criticism and joking when she was seemingly unimpressed with her silver medal (okay, I had to laugh at this too), but at age 15, can we really expect her to just pretend like she's thrilled after such a disappointment? She learned the "performance is dynamic" lesson the hard way.

Even though I am not doing any physical training at the moment, I am certainly exercising my mental muscles by watching these athletes perform and listening to their interviews. I think it's going to be a long road back for me, so I need to keep all of these things in mind once I am able to train again.

CHAPTER 12:
HARD WORK

October 3, 2015

252 people "liked" my Facebook update on Wednesday, and 60 people commented on it. I took a screen shot of my Boston Marathon acceptance email and posted it with this message:

After 7 years and 12 marathons, I finally have this golden ticket. I've never worked so hard for anything else in my entire life. Blood, sweat, and tears cannot begin to describe my journey here.

For many years, I avoided Facebook entirely on "acceptance day" because I couldn't bear to see so many people getting into Boston while I had failed to do so. I was truly happy for my friends who qualified, yet I was overcome with bitterness. Seeing all of the excitement on Facebook didn't inspire me to work harder or change anything. It just filled me with grief and self-pity, and I wasn't able to cope. And now, with 60 congratulatory comments, I realize how many people supported me throughout my journey, while I might have been too consumed with self-pity to reciprocate.

I'm on the other side now. I'm part of the Boston Marathon community. It's an exclusive club that I had felt shut out of for years and years, and had therefore tried to ignore. And now, I'm in.

* * *

All in all, I was out of commission with mono for about three months—from mid-June through mid-September. I made the most of my downtime by absorbing everything that Neal was teaching me and working to change my overall mindset about running.

September 1, 2012

I've always defined myself, in part, by my work ethic. I work very, very hard at things in which I care to succeed. "Working hard" is part of who I am at my core. But now I am realizing that there's more to hard work than what I thought. People work hard at things they are good at. To be truly successful, you need to work hard at things you are not good at.

I consider myself "good" at marathon training because I'm motivated to get out there and do the prescribed workouts. I'm good at making plans and following through. I enjoy structure and following the rules. These are all things that are very easy for me to do because I enjoy them and I've been doing them for a long time. And therefore, it's easy for me to work hard at simply doing the training.

But there are also a slew of other things related to marathon training that I could really improve upon—things that are not easy for me—that may even seem like they aren't even possible:

Making comparisons: I have a tendency to look at other people's race results and immediately compare them to my own. Or look at my results and immediately compare them to other people's results. This is not good for me! Although I am happy for others when they succeed, it's coupled with an "I should be able to do that." When hearing about other people's runs, I need to be happy for their successes and keep that completely, 100%, totally separate from my own running.

Learning from setbacks and moving on: I've gotten better at this over the years, but I am nowhere near where I want to be. It used to be that I just wouldn't learn anything from a poor performance. I'd be upset and it would last for a while. Then I started learning from setbacks, so although I was upset, at least I had something to take away for next time. The problem has always been the moving on part. If I have a bad race, I tend to dwell on it all day, or sometimes even for multiple days. This is not good for me and it will only serve to diminish my confidence. Confidence is critical for good performance, so I can't get caught up in the negative emotions.

Patience*: I am not a patient person. I will work hard for a long time to get good results, but when I know it's time for those results, I can't bear to wait any longer. I have the patience to work through a 16-week training plan, but come race day, I'd better get those results! After each of my "bad" marathons, my first order of business has been to pull out a calendar, find a marathon in 4-6 weeks, and get my result! Right now, I am trying to recover from mono and I have no idea when I will be able to start doing regular training again. Next week? In two weeks? Next month? I would be much better at coping if I had a date that I could count on. I have to work hard at being patient.*

Tempering emotions: *I consider myself to be a very passionate person. It's a part of my personality that I like, but it's not good when negative emotions just consume me. I have always attached emotions to results and outcomes, no matter how hard I worked. I realize that not getting a good result doesn't diminish the hard work, but the disappointment that comes from not getting the desired result always overshadows the pride from doing the work. I need to work hard at attaching pride and positive emotions to the process and the work. A sub-par marathon time doesn't change the fact that I spent the past 16 weeks waking up at 5:00 a.m. and running my butt off every day!*

Expecting to make mistakes: *Whenever I make a mistake, I feel the need to fix it immediately. I am not okay with making mistakes. I apologize profusely at work or to other people if the mistake somehow affected them. And I try hard to make up for it. At my* *previous job mistakes weren't tolerated, and I was there for so long that it felt normal to me. But at my new job, people don't make a big deal out of mistakes. It's expected. We're only human—we're working on a hundred things at once under tight deadlines, so mistakes happen. I'd love for my "internal culture" to shift along with the way my work environment culture has shifted. Work hard, expect great things out of yourself, but also expect to make mistakes and not make a huge deal out of them.*

I am going to focus on these five things (maybe not all at once) and I think that once I do, I will be a happier person overall and I will find more success in anything I strive for, not just running marathons. I really need to start thinking more about this list, using my discipline to work hard at each one, and accepting that I will be out of my comfort zone. I will have to correct a lot of bad habits and mentally train myself to have a different outlook. The byproduct of NOT working hard at this list is a great deal of anxiety, which ultimately comes back to bite me come race day. Telling myself to simply relax won't cut it. I need to work hard at the things I'm uncomfortable with.

* * *

I resumed running in mid-September, which gave me about two months to prepare for the Richmond Half Marathon. I was careful not to do too much too soon, as I did not want to relapse back into the illness. I continued to see Neal on a weekly basis, and I remained fully committed to working on changing my mindset. Even though having mono was certainly no walk in the park, it happened at the best possible time. It allowed me to truly take a step back from running, and when I returned, I was able to "practice" focusing on the process of running, as opposed to trying to set PRs with each race.

I was looking at running through a new lens, and I took every opportunity I could find to apply the principles that Neal was teaching me. When the New York City Marathon was cancelled due to Hurricane Sandy, there was a wide range of reactions among runners.

November 4, 2012

One of the common themes I am hearing from the various articles on the NYC Marathon cancellation is that runners have made a huge investment in their training. The word "investment" is interesting to me because I've been working hard to move away from "investment model" running.

Investment model running is the attitude that you put "x" amount of time and effort into training to receive "y" result on race day. I've held this attitude for years and years—in fact, ever since I started racing back in 2005. It's just always seemed logical to me. To set a PR or run a specific time, you need to invest the time and hard work. And on race day, it will all pay off.

But this notion of the race somehow "paying you back" actually is not all that logical when you really think about it. And it does a disservice to all your hard work. A race result speaks to how you performed on one day in one set of conditions. I'm not going to say race results aren't important—they do matter—at least to me. However, if you're training with the idea that "this will all pay off," then you risk huge disappointment if, say, the race gets canceled, and more importantly, you're also missing out on the joy and satisfaction that comes with simply doing the training.

For years I've been going into races with the mindset that the race was going to pay me back. Oftentimes it didn't, and I was crushed. Although I have always gotten a great deal of satisfaction from my training, it was always secondary to the end result. "I trained hard and enjoyed my training, BUT I bonked at the marathon." And the second part of that sentence was really where all my emotion was focused. No amount of telling myself that I worked hard and trained hard would make me feel better about performing poorly at a marathon.

Investment model running simply isn't effective or realistic. It can often lead to disappointment, and you miss out on the stuff that truly matters in terms of your athleticism.

Keeping this in mind, I've developed some goals for the Richmond Half Marathon next weekend. What do I want to get out of this race if it's not payback for my training/comeback over the last 5 weeks? I think what I really want to do in Richmond is demonstrate that I can effectively do some of the mental stuff I've been working on. Although my performance anxiety issues only come with marathons and not half marathons, I want to go into all races with the same attitude—no matter what the distance or the priority level.

1. Do not compare myself to others. *This will be very challenging to me, especially since Richmond was supposed to be my fall marathon this year. Many of my Capital Area Runners friends are running this race and so is Greg. It would be very easy to fall into negative thinking about how they get to run the full marathon and set PRs, but I was stuck with mono all summer. Comparing to others will not only make me feel badly about myself, but it's also completely illogical. I don't know anyone else who got stuck with mono all summer, so why would I compare myself to them?*

2. Focus on the present. *The race starts on Saturday morning, and ends 13.1 miles later. The night before the race, I will be enjoying dinner with Greg and my CAR friends. During that dinner, I will not be thinking about my race performance. Talking about the race in terms of the course, the logistics, etc., is fine, but I want to be present at the dinner and not off in my own mind, worrying about the race.*

When I'm done racing, I will do a quick review of it in my head and make some mental notes. Afterwards, I will be focused on cheering for Greg and the other marathoners. When Greg finishes the marathon, I will be focused on supporting him. We'll of course exchange stories of how it went, but my goal here is to not obsess over my performance. When I get home, I will write my race recap blog and do an official "review" in the style of what went well, what worked, what I learned, etc. And then, it's time to focus on celebrating my birthday!

3. Focus on my race strategy and execution. *Here are the key areas where I want to be focused on immediately before and during the race:*

- *Run the first 5K relaxed, and slower than half marathon pace*
- *Stay physically relaxed, don't tense up*

- *Focus on form, especially on the hills*
- *Take gels at miles 4 and 9*
- *Look at the Garmin once in a while, but stay focused on actually running!*
- *Stay mentally strong during the last 4 miles. You can do this! Don't back off.*
- *Really kick it hard on that final downhill mile*

All that being said, I do have a target range of where I'd like to be in terms of time. This will guide my pacing during the first 5K and ensure that I don't go out too fast. These three goals will be far more challenging for me than attaining any particular race time. And I love a challenge! The good thing is that they are all within my grasp and control, so there is no reason why I can't achieve them.

Moving away from investment model running feels liberating, but it's not an overnight shift. To be completely honest, it's unfamiliar territory and scary at times. I've always clung so tightly to my race times to validate my training. The more I set these types of goals, and demonstrate that I can achieve them, the more natural it will become.

* * *

The Richmond Half Marathon ended up going well for me. I accomplished all of the goals I set out for myself and finished in 1:46:19. Ten weeks prior, I hadn't even been able to walk around my neighborhood at a normal walking pace. I had also been afraid that I would never recover, or that I would never be the same runner I was before the illness.

I knew that I had worked hard over the previous several months to stay positive, redefine what I see as an "accomplishment," and to physically get myself back into shape. It all came together for me in Richmond, and I was proud of myself.

In addition to the race going well, I gained a renewed focus on what was truly important to me, and what some of my core values were. This went back to what Neal had asked me to do at the beginning—to define myself by my beliefs and my guiding principles, not by my achievements.

After I finished the race, I found one of my Capital Area Runners friends in the finish line festival area. We walked to the baggage check area together, where we met up with three other runners from CAR. This was the group of women that I had trained with before I got sick. Previously, we had all trained and raced at around the same pace, but having mono obviously set me back quite a bit. Everyone was very excited and they were sharing their times with each other and with me. They all set impressive PRs, and most of them ran sub-1:40 races for the first time.

I didn't say anything about my race or my time, but I told them that I needed to get my checked bag. As I stood in line at the nearby baggage truck, the four of them started to walk away—they were going to cheer on the marathoners. It was like they had forgotten that I existed. One of them, however, turned around and told me that they were going to mile marker 17, and that I should meet them there. It was a nice gesture, but not very helpful given that I had no clue where mile marker 17 was, and I didn't have a course map.

Being left alone at the baggage truck was definitely a buzz kill. I was already trying hard not to compare my time to theirs and to be happy with my own personal accomplishment. But the fact that they couldn't wait an extra few minutes for me to get my bag made me feel like they simply didn't care about me. In reality, they probably were just more focused on seeing some of the faster marathons pass through mile 17 than they were on making sure everyone in the group was ready to go together.

I discussed this incident with Neal, who told me not to take it personally, and ultimately I got over it. Holding onto negative emotions wasn't doing me any good. But I did learn something valuable. Instead of feeling sorry for myself and being upset with those four women, I took the opportunity to take a closer look at myself and my core values. What type of person was I? A good person, doing good things? Well, yes, actually. I was thoughtful, empathetic, and sensitive to other peoples' feelings. I realized that these core values were what defined me—not the races that I ran.

* * *

As I focused so much of my mental energy on learning how to have a more balanced mindset about running, thoughts of qualifying for Boston faded into the background. However, it was definitely still a goal of mine. My next marathon would be the B & A Trail Marathon in Maryland in mid-March. I had heard about this small race from several of my running friends and it had an excellent reputation. The course was a paved "rails to trails" biking and running path that was primarily flat with only one major hill. I was done with the Shamrock Marathon, and this small, 300-person race seemed like it would be conducive to helping me relax. I would be turning 35 in the fall, which meant that I'd have an extra five minutes to qualify for Boston so my target once again was 3:40.

The further away I got from my mono experience, the stronger and fitter I became. By the time January rolled around, I was positioned for a great year of running. As I resumed my normal training regime with the Capital Area Runners, I continued to work with Neal on setting realistic goals and expectations for myself.

As a "recovering perfectionist," I was learning that I tended to set the bar too high. Previously, I would go into the majority of my races expecting PRs. I always thought this was a good thing because I wanted to set the bar high. I wanted to push myself. But now I was realizing that pushing myself didn't mean setting the bar high for every race in terms of a time goal.

There are three "levels" of performance, according to Neal. I could run the best race I had in me on race day, and end up in any one of these three areas:

1. The "bottom line." This is the range of times I would get if things didn't really go my way. I might expect to fall into my bottom line range if the weather were hot, if I were coming off of an injury, if I just didn't "feel it" that day, if my nutrition or hydration were off. There are many reasons why I might run in this bottom line range.

2. The "mid-range" area. If things generally went well during a race, I'd land in the mid-range.

3. The "upper end" area. This is where the PR and beyond lives. I should only expect to be in this range if I had an amazing day, where everything came together. This includes my training, the ability to execute my strategy, and things beyond my control like the weather.

In a given year, how often could I expect to be at #3? Previously, I had expected that more than 50% of my races would be at #3. This wasn't realistic—at least not for someone who had been running for as long as I had been. For experienced runners who are past the point of setting PRs at each race, it's realistic to be at #3 about 20% of the time. Neal told me that "normal" and "realistic" for experienced runners was 50% at the bottom line, 30% in the mid-range, and 20% at the upper end.

Neal also said that if he were to interview the first 1,000 finishers of a large race, probably 20% of them would have set PRs, 30% would have been in their mid-range, and half of them would have been at their bottom line. This was an eye opener for me.

Neal asked me to think about what specific ranges of times I would put in each bucket for 2013. The ultimate goal of training was to lower all of the ranges, but this wouldn't happen overnight. I shouldn't be revising these buckets every time I raced—I needed to be focused on the big picture of my running as opposed to any one specific race. Based on this framework, I started to set goals for 2013.

One of my many New Year's resolutions was to set the bar high for myself in a completely different way. Instead of always trying to set PRs, I decided to work toward:

- Believing in myself and my ability to work hard
- Keeping running separate from other areas of my life
- Conducting constructive post-race reviews and weekly training reviews
- Having patience
- Letting myself run without judgment
- Focusing on the process of running a race, as opposed to the outcome

- Attaching emotions to the process (ex: being happy about executing my race strategy)

I also used the New Year as an opportunity to take a step back and see how far I had come during the seven months that I had been working with Neal:

January 4, 2013

I need to understand that at my level, PRs are the exception, not the rule. I need to go into races less focused on time, and more focused on how I will run the race. This "setting the bar" is not so much about goal setting, but being realistic about how I review my performances afterward. Running the best race I can on a particular day does not necessarily equal a PR.

I'm now much better at separating my running from who I am as a person. I never did this before because I didn't think it was important. Actually, I thought that all successful runners were completely defined by their sport and ate, breathed, and slept it. I've opened my eyes and taken a good look around me and realized that the most successful athletes I know are not defined by their running. It's just one aspect of their life and they aren't carrying it into conversations at parties or into the workday, or letting it just occupy their mind 24/7.

I've learned to focus on the big picture of my running as opposed to any one individual race. Marathon training is generally focused around one goal race, and all the workouts, etc. are timed accordingly. Therefore, it's hard not to see the marathon as the "A" race of the season and everything else as "B" and "C." But I really want to put everything on a level playing field. No one race defines my training cycle. And there aren't races that are "just for fun" and "for time." Every race should be fun. And I should care about my time for every race, although not have it be the main focus.

Will I qualify for Boston? Absolutely, I know I will. Will it be the next marathon I run? I don't know. I'm focusing now on the bigger picture of my running, and I won't let one race—one day— be the judgment of weeks and months and years of hard work and dedication.

I think that I have progressed more as an athlete in 2012 than in any other year. By having mono, I gained new perspective and was able to "practice" skills that would be hard to learn if I were in peak condition physically. With all of this in mind, I am ready to embrace whatever 2013 will bring.

PART V

A BREAKTHROUGH

CHAPTER 13:
EVIDENCE

One of the most commonly used words in my blog was "proof." I needed to prove to myself and to others that my claim of being fast enough for Boston was a valid one. If I set a PR in a non-marathon distance, like my 1:41:40 half marathon, I would see it as "proof" that I was Boston-worthy. I thought that finding proof in my training paces and other races would result in confidence, but it actually resulted in more pressure. It raised my expectations of how fast I could run a marathon. Even though I had only ever "proved" myself capable of a 3:51, I thought that I also had proof that I was a 3:35 marathoner.

A more appropriate word is "evidence." True confidence is built on evidence that something is possible. Anxiety is rooted in a false sense of proof and entitlement. I thought I deserved to run Boston (the word "deserve" was another common word in my blog) based solely on how hard I trained and my resulting fitness level. I was missing a huge piece of the puzzle, however, and that was execution. I was far more focused on the outcome of my races than I was on the process of running them. If I had looked for *evidence* that I could execute according to plan as opposed to *proof* that I could produce a certain result, I would have been far less anxious.

* * *

I ran two half marathons in preparation for the B & A Trail
Marathon. One was the Walt Disney World Half Marathon in
January, and the other was the Love Rox Half Marathon in
February. Greg and I thought it would be fun to make a mini-
vacation out of the Disney World Half Marathon, and we
thoroughly enjoyed our time there. The race weather was
challenging—low 60's and very humid. In spite of that, I ran a
1:43:48, which was my second fastest half marathon to date. I
mainly just focused on staying strong throughout the race and
giving it all that I had. It was great practice for the tools that Neal
was teaching me.

The Love Rox Half Marathon provided even more of an
opportunity to hone these skills. I wrote a blog post about it that
received a record number of views.

February 16, 2013

*I have this recurring dream where I'm running a race and
it turns into an obstacle course, and then I somehow get lost. I
think I'm winning the race, when the truth is that I'm just going the
wrong way. The most common obstacle is a staircase, and when I
get lost, nobody is around to tell me where to go. That dream came
true, in part, this morning at the Love Rox Half Marathon in
Richmond.*

*I registered for this race about three weeks ago, per the
advice of my coach. He likes the idea of running a half marathon
tune-up race four weeks out from a goal marathon. Love Rox in
Richmond was perfectly timed for this, and with a 10:00 a.m. start,
I could drive down the morning of the race without having to deal
with a hotel.*

*Being the inaugural year, I thought there might be some
hiccups. However, the organization that was hosting the race had
a good reputation for organizing triathlons. The race website
seemed very professional and it had a fun Valentine's Day theme,
with elements such as "proposal hot spots" along the course where
you could propose to your loved one during the race.*

*The course description was also very attractive. The
website advertised, "The course is very flat with the exception of*

some small gradual inclines up to the Lee Bridge and a few short steps down to the Canal Walk." I raised my eyebrows at the "short steps down" part, but I thought I could handle a few steps down during a half marathon. I went into the race a tad skeptical, but open-minded and optimistic about what the course would bring.

There was a huge printout of the course map on site, in which the start line had been moved. This seemed like a last-minute change because it hadn't been communicated via email or on the website. I wondered why they moved it and what that meant for the course distance, but nobody seemed to know.

I found my CAR teammates Jessica and Patricia, who were also skeptical about the course and organization. We said we were just going to "go with it" whatever it ended up being, but we weren't expecting greatness from the course.

The race website advertised chip timing, which I interpret to mean a starting mat and a finishing mat. Well, the new start line wasn't actually a start line. They gathered us all onto a grassy area and told us to stand between two cones. It ended up being an extremely wide start, and we'd all eventually end up running on a path after just 0.1 mile on the grass. (Oh yeah, and running on grass is another part of my recurring race dream. I hate doing it.)

They counted down from five and then the horn honked. I just couldn't believe how ridiculous this start was, but I figured I'd be on a nice course soon and the "bizarre race" feeling would end.

We started running and maybe about half a mile into it, we ran down a staircase, and then up a staircase. These were not small staircases or "short steps" by any stretch of the imagination. I didn't think this was right because I thought we would just run down a staircase—not immediately back up another one, too. We got to the top, and I was just running along starting to get into a groove post-staircase when I noticed that the people ahead of me didn't know where to go. The leaders started yelling out, "Where do we go?" Seriously, nobody knew where the course was.

Finally, we realized we had to go back down the staircase, and we never should have gone up it to begin with. So in addition to the four "planned" staircase runs, a lack of direction made us run six staircases, and definitely lengthened the course. By the time I saw mile marker 1, my Garmin read 10:00. (The plan was to go out at a pace of around 7:45-7:50.)

Everyone seemed so pissed about this. I actually thought that they would declare it a false start, stop the race and have everyone start over. That would have been a good thing, but no, the race continued. At that point, I pretty much knew a PR wouldn't be happening unless I somehow made up that time. I stayed optimistic and continued running.

We ran underneath a railroad track and a bridge, so the Garmin got all wacky. I had thought that even if I didn't get an accurate time due to the course screw-up, at least I'd have good Garmin data. Well, not true. My Garmin data for this race was all over the map. And if you include miles with staircases, I ran those probably about 10-15 seconds per mile slower than if there had been no staircase.

It was cold (upper 30's) and raining. We weren't running on asphalt but other surfaces, like the sidewalk that's made out of those little rocks. And concrete. And there were tons of potholes everywhere. Someone posted on the race's Facebook wall afterwards: "The ducking through the flood wall was awkward. The potholes and uneven terrain made injuries a serious concern." I agree—the course was not safe for several reasons. The terrain was just a small part of that.

I stuck with Jessica and Patricia during these miles and we were taking it all in stride. We hit a water station and Patricia couldn't get water. I was holding a bottle, so this didn't affect me, but she literally had to stop and wait for someone to get her water. This happened multiple times throughout the race. There were not enough volunteers, and the ones who were there didn't seem to be paying attention.

Up another staircase and we were finally on what seemed to be a typical race course. I lagged behind Patricia and Jessica on the staircase and didn't catch up to them afterwards. The gap between me and them got wider and wider, and I started to get frustrated and lose confidence. Physically, I just felt like I was expending way too much effort to be at mile 5 of a half marathon, and mentally I was drained from how horribly the course was designed. As I watched Patricia and Jessica fade away in the distance, I had some interesting self-talk:

I think I'm just going to drop out. The time I get won't be an accurate reflection of where I am fitness-wise, which is one of the main purposes of a tune-up race. I feel like shit. I don't want to have to run a second loop of this exhausting course. There is no way I will be able to maintain this pace for the rest of the race. This just isn't my day. When I see Greg at mile 7, I'm just going to call it quits. I'll still have legs fresh enough to do a long run tomorrow and salvage some training for this weekend. This course is a joke and it's not worth my effort.

What do I really want out of this race anyway? And that question made me think. Seriously think. All these months working with a sports psychologist, trying to focus on the process and not the outcome. And then the question became a good one—what can I get out of this race? What will I miss out on if I quit?

A lot! I'm not running this race with the sole purpose of a PR. I want to prove to myself that I can push hard when things get tough. I want this run to boost my confidence for future races. Even if my time sucks, I want to feel like I put out my best effort. Quitting is not my best effort. I am going to surge now and start putting forth some serious effort. I might crash later on, but I am going to push for it now! I'm going to race this one!

At that point, I put my foot on the gas and started passing people. I sped up quite a bit and the gap between Patricia and me was getting smaller and smaller. At one point, I passed a guy who said to me, "Where are you going?" I laughed and then sped by. All of a sudden I felt energized. I felt good again!

I am so proud of myself. I just proved to myself that I can turn a negative attitude into a positive one by focusing on the process (not the race result), and by doing so, make myself feel better physically. It's amazing how much my improved mental state made me feel. I was peppy again and excited to be in a race.

I found this course to be unsafe at many points. The road was not closed off to cars, so we had to run on a sidewalk. Some people were running on the road anyway, myself included. I kept on passing people and surging ahead until I finally caught up with Patricia. Yay! It was great to be running with her, and I was able to feed off of her positive energy.

After mile marker 7, I knew to expect Greg, who was waiting for me with a replacement water bottle. I later learned that he was also helping out as a course marshal, directing people on where to go. Since they were so light on volunteers and people didn't know where to go, he was actually directing people. One person actually made a rude comment to him, as if he were part of the course management.

This race also had a 10K, which ran one loop of the course, but started at 10:45. This means that Patricia and I got to spend our entire second loop passing slower 10K runners. This might not have been an issue if we weren't forced onto narrow sidewalks and if there wasn't a portion that was an out-and-back, further crowding the course. It was really mentally draining to have to constantly be passing people.

Patricia and I couldn't really run side-by-side because we had to keep passing other people. Even still, we kept each other in check, encouraging each other to stay strong and that we didn't have much farther to go. It started to sleet during the last two miles, which made things even more interesting, especially on hills. We had already done these monstrous hills on loop one and now we had to conquer them a second time, right at the end of the race. I toughed it out and stayed strong, screaming all the way down the hill because I thought I would fall over.

At the bottom of the hill, about 30 feet before the finish line, we had the privilege of running over some serious cobblestone. It wasn't a long stretch, just enough to make you slow down considerably during what should be a final kick. We crossed the finish line (there was no timing mat), and I was so grateful to be done with that race.

I met up with Greg, who had a big bouquet of roses for me! I am so happy I actually finished the race because I would have felt guilty if I hadn't. We were curious about age group awards (not realizing there were people who only ran 10 miles who would be skewing them anyway). We couldn't tell from the results if we won anything, but we suspected we didn't. My name actually didn't even appear in the results. I finished a few seconds behind Patricia, and her time was 1:43:xx, but there was no record of me. My Garmin read 13.34, and I think Patricia's read 13.4. Another teammate had 13.5. Sigh.

I actually got a lot out of this race. A lot more than I would have thought, given the crappy organization and course.

- *I've proven to myself that I can get over a mental slump in a race.*
- *I've proven that getting over a mental slump also makes me feel better physically, and I can speed up when I am already thinking I am at full effort.*
- *I can put forth a solid effort and run a strong performance, even when I know a PR is out of the question.*
- *When things don't go as expected, I can adapt and make adjustments.*
- *I hit my "sweet spot" at around mile 6 of a half marathon, so I shouldn't worry if I am not "feeling it" before then.*
- *When things get tough during a race, I can remind myself what I am capable of physically and do it.*

I have no official time, splits that are inaccurate and slower than they would be on a non-staircase course, and definitely no PR. But I ran very strong. Some of my miles clocked in as fast as 7:16. Others were closer to 8:00 due to staircases and hills. I was completely inconsistent pace-wise, but very consistent effort-wise once I made the decision that I was going to try my best. A very valuable learning experience, and I'm glad I raced this one. Would I do it again next year? Definitely not.

* * *

As the B & A Trail Marathon drew closer, I started to realize that most of my anxiety issues stemmed from not knowing how the race was going to play out. Was I going to bonk? Would I meet my goal time? What would my splits look like?

Neal asked me if all of this was really such an unknown, and advised me to focus on the things that I was certain of. For the things that I couldn't predict, he told me to have a plan for how to handle them if they went badly. The "What If" game had always caused me so much stress. What if the weather was too hot? What if I started to cramp? What if I bonked again? Neal said that the "What If" game was actually a helpful tool if used properly. It ensured that I had a plan for responding to the unknowns on race day, so I wouldn't have to worry about them beforehand. What did I know about B &A?

- I knew everything that I was going to do on race morning before the race started.
- I knew what the course was like because I had studied the map.
- I knew what pace I was going to start at, and I had a plan to speed up once I hit the 10K point.
- I knew that I would see Greg cheering for me along the course and that he would hand me water and gels.
- I knew that that at some point the race would start to feel hard and that I would need to continue to push through it.
- I knew that barring any stomach issues or injuries, I would finish the race.

March 9, 2013

Of course there were a few things I can't predict. I don't know how I will feel and at what point the race will start to get tough. I don't know if I will have stomach issues. I can't predict what my splits will be or what my finish time will be. But I'm trying to become more comfortable with these unknowns. After all, if I knew exactly how everything would go on race day, there would be no excitement in racing.

It's been five years since I've had a strong marathon finish, but I don't feel like I am "due." It will happen when it's meant to happen. And it hasn't happened within the past five years for a reason. A marathon time goal is far less significant than all the other goals I am working on this year. I'm working on overhauling a perfectionist mindset that I've had my entire life. Showing progress in that area is far more meaningful to me than a race result.

I have a great deal of evidence to show that I can be happy, proud, and satisfied when a race doesn't go as well as I would have liked. The Love Rox Half Marathon is perhaps the best example of that. I also have evidence that focusing on doing my best will make me feel physically and mentally strong during a race. I feel ready for this marathon.

* * *

In spite of all of the hard work I had been doing for the previous nine months to reduce my race anxiety, it came back in full force during the week leading up to B & A. A week before the race, on a Sunday night, I was unable to sleep. I was up for the entire night for no apparent reason. My appointment with Neal wasn't until Wednesday, but I wanted to see him on Monday, and he thankfully had an available spot. Neal and I identified the many reasons why I wasn't able to sleep, but the important takeaway was that one night wasn't evidence of a pattern.

"One of anything is not indicative of a larger trend," said Neal. "If something happens repeatedly, and you start to notice a pattern, then it's probably worth exploring. But there's no need to worry about something that happens just once."

I tried to just brush it off and not worry about it, as Neal advised, but then I didn't sleep well on Monday night either. I only got 3-4 hours of off-and-on sleep, and during that time I just felt so tortured.

Finally, on Tuesday night, I slept for seven hours. While I was hoping to have slept even longer to make up for Sunday and Monday, I was happy to not have had another tortured night. Despite having slept, I had a huge knot in my chest when I woke up on Wednesday morning. I tried to ignore it, but the more I tried to ignore it, the tighter it felt.

Greg and I went for a 4-mile run, and my heart rate was elevated by 15 beats per minute. I was running at an 8:45 pace, but my heart rate monitor indicated that I was putting forth about a 7:30 effort. This freaked me out even more, and I continued on a downward spiral from there. I had an elevated heart rate, a knot in my stomach, and I hadn't slept well for the previous two nights. I was a mess. There was nothing I could do to make it stop. I tried crying, talking it out with Greg, meditating, and praying, but I still felt physically wound up.

At that point, I decided I wasn't even going to run the race. It wasn't worth all of the physical anxiety. I was just going to call it quits before I even started. I hadn't expected that I would feel like this in the week leading up to the race, and it upset me. I had worked so hard over the past nine months addressing my "perfectionist" attitude about marathons, and yet I was still getting knots in my chest and not sleeping.

Finally, Greg was able to talk me down from my state of distress and I felt much better. "Your goal shouldn't be to eliminate the anxiety," Greg said. "The important thing is how you react to it and manage it." He was right. Once again, focusing on things I *could* control instead of those I couldn't was the best course of action. Slowly, the knot in my chest went away and I got ready to go to work.

I saw Neal again on Wednesday night, and he gave me some great advice on how to focus my thoughts during the next few days. I needed to focus on the things I could control, and not let this anxiety become a self-fulfilling prophecy. (Of course, this is pretty much what Greg had told me that morning, but hearing it reinforced by a professional was helpful.) I needed to work on not letting my anxiety turn into even more anxiety by simply accepting it when it hit.

By Thursday I felt better. During my run, my heart rate was elevated by only five beats per minute. This was still not ideal, but it proved that I was able to lower it from the previous day. Knowing that I had the power to lower it gave me hope and made me feel more in control. I wore the heart rate monitor while running, but I didn't look at the numbers until post-run, which was a good idea.

Although I had a horrible start to the race week, I was able to get myself back on track instead of continuing the downward spiral. I slept decently Thursday night, and woke up feeling good on Friday morning.

Greg and I drove to Annapolis on Friday evening, and before I knew it, it was time to run my 14th marathon. Greg was recovering from an injury and wasn't running the race as originally planned. This allowed him to run the first few miles of the race with me with the goal of helping me relax. I recapped the race in my blog as such:

March 16, 2013

Greg and I started the race slowly. I didn't even bother looking at the Garmin to gauge my pace for the first mile—I just wanted to run easy. I enjoyed these early miles. The weather was perfect— overcast and 43. It was nice to be running in a new area. To ease my anxiety, Greg and I pretended we were doing a training run. We even joked about how there were water stops on our training run. And how people on our training run were wearing race bibs. Laughing and chatting away made the miles tick by quickly and distracted me from what I was really doing.

Mile 1: 8:53
Mile 2: 8:59
Mile 3: 8:31
Mile 4: 8:36
Mile 5: 8:29

I knew that I was over the initial hump and I was still feeling good, so all signs were pointing toward a strong race. I turned my music on and let it carry me. I got into a groove and everything felt awesome. I had a huge smile on my face. I high-fived the little kids, I said thanks to the volunteers, and I just soaked it all in. The weather was perfect, the course was nice, and it was an amazing experience. This is why I run marathons. I used to get this feeling back in 2006-2007 when I was new to marathons, but ever since I decided I wanted to BQ, I'd taken myself too seriously to high-five the kids or "waste" the energy to thank the volunteers.

Mile 6: 8:35
Mile 7: 8:20
Mile 8: 8:21
Mile 9: 8:26
Mile 10: 8:18
Mile 11: 8:26

Greg was waiting for me where I expected and I breezed by him, taking the second bottle of G2 sports drink. The music was still motivating me. I was still running strong. I looked at the Garmin about 1-2 times per mile to check on my pace, which is a lot less than I usually do. I realized that the paces I was running probably weren't going to get me to a BQ, but I wanted to play it safe given my lack of sleep that week. I wanted to avoid a crash at all costs. And I knew that if I still felt good later in the race, I could just turn on the gas during the last 10K and make up the time there.

Mile 12: 8:26
Mile 13: 8:31
Mile 14: 8:38
Mile 15: 8:22
Mile 16: 8:18
Mile 17: 8:34

I came upon a long-awaited water station at mile 18. I was thirsty so I quickly gulped down two cups of water. I prepared to take my 3rd Honey Stinger gel (which I had ideally wanted at mile 16, but there was no water there), and the minute I put it in my mouth I felt like I was going to vomit, so I spit it out. I stayed at that water station for a full minute. Stopping there for so long may have been a mistake because it made me realize that I no longer felt good. I suddenly felt a sharp pain in my chest which made me feel like I needed to vomit.

The next few miles were hellish. I went into survival mode. I didn't try to think about what caused it; I just did my best to power through it and prayed that it would go away soon. I kept burping, and each burp felt like a release, but the pain was still there. In retrospect, I think a number of things could have contributed. It could have been anxiety-related (it was in the same area where I had felt that knot in my chest earlier in the week). It could have been from drinking too much G2 early in the race, and no water. It could have been from gulping down the cups of water too quickly.

Regardless, the unfortunate thing was that I hadn't consumed any calories since mile 14, and with the way I was feeling, I knew it would be nearly impossible to take any more in. I expected to see Greg shortly after mile 20 and I wanted to look good for him. I put on my best game face, but I walked as I approached him, threw down my gloves and my hat, and took a sip of water. The water made me feel like I needed to gag. UGH! I didn't even say anything to Greg other than that I couldn't drink the water. I walked away, and then slowly resumed running.

Mile 18: 8:24
Mile 19: 9:40
Mile 20: 9:10
Mile 21: 9:21
Mile 22: 9:40
Mile 23: 9:40

At this point, I told myself, "You are going to run to mile marker 24. And then you will run to mile marker 25. And then, marker 26." I didn't think of it as three more miles. I thought of it as manageable chunks of distance. Thinking about it like this was very helpful and gradually, my chest/stomach problem started to dissipate. Instead of getting frustrated and discouraged about how this was impacting my time, I powered through it, determined to have a strong finish. In the past, I think I probably would have given up mentally and turned it into more of a catastrophe than it needed to be. Plus, even though I was struggling, I was still passing people.

I looked down at my Garmin and realized I could still PR. My average pace per mile was 8:44 and my PR pace per mile was 8:49. I was determined to get it. With two miles left to go, I came upon someone who was hanging in there, but obviously going slower than me. I said something encouraging to him as I passed. Before I knew it, he was by my side and we were running together. Yay! I had someone to run with. I kept saying "We got this," and my big smile returned. I knew that things were only going to get better as I felt strong again and my chest pain was now just a minor annoyance.

I cannot emphasize enough how great it felt to be feeling strong at the end of a marathon. I haven't had a strong marathon finish since March of 2008. It's been five years. It was euphoric. It didn't matter that my time would be slower than what I was physically capable of. All that mattered was that I was going to finish happy and strong, and that I was pulling someone else with me.

"I see mile marker 26!" I exclaimed like a giddy child. With even more newfound energy, we ran to mile 26 and then I realized that if I sprinted I could get under 3:49. I ran that last 0.2 like the

end of a 10K and my final kick was awesome. It was so awesome that I felt like I could have kept going. In fact, I think that if the race had been 28 miles, my overall average pace would have been faster. Ironic, but true, since I had plenty of energy and my legs felt good.

Mile 24: 9:01
Mile 25: 8:55
Mile 26: 8:23
Last 0.2: (7:43 pace)

My legs felt great toward the end, so I guess all of the training prepared me well after all! My time was 3:48:50,which was good for 3rd female, ages 30-39. It was a small race.

I found Greg and he said, "You look much better now than when I saw you last!" I was so happy! I haven't felt so satisfied with a marathon in years! And the funny thing is—if I had run a 3:48 last year at this time, I would have been crushed. If I had the exact same race experience, I would have been upset that I didn't qualify for Boston despite how great my fitness level was and how hard I trained. It wouldn't have mattered that I broke 3:50 for the first time, or that I beat my PR by over 2:00. It would have been a depressing day of "this is so unfair, why can't I just run a good marathon." But not today. I was fulfilled in so many ways.

The age group award and the PR were just the gravy in this race. I am most proud of how I conquered my pre-race anxiety and got to the start line feeling relaxed. This resulted in a strong, happy finish and an affirmation that I have made some major fitness gains over the past few months—especially coming back from mono last summer.

I can't help but wonder what would have happened if I pushed a bit more before the stomach issues. I'm not thinking about that in terms of what I did wrong, but just for next time I would like to have more confidence and be a bit less conservative. This race was not focused on speed or testing my fitness—it was about refining the process. I've made huge progress and I now know what I need to do next time.

CHAPTER 14:
BOSTON STRONG

One year after the 2013 bombings, The Harvard Kennedy School released a report titled *"Why* was Boston Strong?," analyzing the response to the attacks.

"Senior leaders [of response organizations] should not be unduly exposed to the enormous flow of raw information, lest their attention be diverted from strategic issues and problems," states the report as one of its key findings. I think this statement applies more broadly to mental strength. Mentally strong people are focused on the big picture of what they are doing, and are not distracted by potentially irrelevant information.

In order to overcome my mental barriers and qualify for Boston, I needed to rid myself of irrelevant distractions: other people's marathon times, what other people thought of me, the number of hours I slept each night, the "enormous flow" of raw data from my training log, and other streams of other unnecessary noise that made a peaceful existence impossible. The constant worry and obsession prevented me from doing what I needed to do to run a strong race: relax.

Neal says that we most clearly remember experiences that have strong emotions attached to them. We don't remember the minute details of our day-to-day lives; we remember the moments that made us feel particularly delighted, surprised, scared, sad, frustrated, or any other strong emotion.

To perform well, though, the key is to not be overwhelmed by feelings. During the performance, successful athletes forget about what they like, what they don't like, what makes them happy or sad, and focus completely on the task at hand. Things that could cause them to become emotional don't distract them. During the performance, they are emotion-neutral.

The emotion comes when the performance is complete. Neal refers to this as "later fun." When I think about my most recent races, I remember the mechanics of them and how I executed them. In fact, I remember very little about my Boston qualifying race, except for the fact that I was focused on pushing hard the entire time. Running is a simple sport. Once I was able to clear my mind of all the unnecessary junk I was holding on to, running became so much easier.

But I don't run so that I can feel "neutral." I run for the satisfaction of achievement, and for the joy of engaging in the sport. I run for enjoyment, excitement, and empowerment. Realistically, I know that there will be races in the future that don't go as planned, and I won't feel any of these positive emotions. The key is to try to focus on the positive elements and learnings, and know that it's okay to be disappointed. According to Neal, disappointment is the only negative feeling that I should ever logically feel after a race. Why would I feel frustrated, sad, or angry . . . ever? It's easy to recover from disappointment, move on, and focus on the next race.

* * *

When the Boston Marathon bombings occurred on April 15, 2013, I received calls, emails, and text messages from concerned friends, asking me if I was in Boston and if I was okay. It was a nice reminder that I had a solid network of people who cared about me. At the same time, I was closely watching Facebook and waiting for my friends in Boston to post that they were safe.

It also gave me an outside-in perspective on my running. In my mind, not having qualified for Boston was this huge strike against me—like I was walking around with a black eye. There were the "haves" and the "have-nots" of the running world, and I was clearly a "have not." But from an outside perspective, many of my friends simply knew that I liked to run, and that I could have potentially been running the Boston Marathon on April 15.

My immediate reaction to the text messages and emails was to say, "I haven't qualified for Boston yet, so no—I am not there." But instead I took it in stride and simply told them I was safe at home. In light of the fact that a bomb critically injured people, my BQ insecurities seemed insignificant.

As the spring training season drew to a close, I used Neal's framework to reflect positively on my accomplishments. Even though I had been working with him for a full year, there was still an internal battle going on inside my head. The "new me" was trying to view my racing season in a positive light, but the perfectionist "old me" wanted to criticize it and feel sorry for myself. I wrote down all of the thoughts that "perfectionist Elizabeth" was thinking, and challenged each one with the perspective I wanted to have.

Old me: *Even though I was in the best shape of my life, I only got one PR this season.*
New me: *My one PR was the marathon, which is what I have been working toward for years.*

Old me: *The marathon PR I got was nice, but it was small, and I still didn't perform to my full physical capacity.*
New me: *The marathon PR is a huge victory—it was my first PR in four years! I finished the race strongly and worked hard to deal with my race anxiety. It's unrealistic to expect that after years of anxiety-ridden races, I am just going to break out of it suddenly with a 3:35. My mental abilities still need to catch up with my physical abilities and I am showing progress.*

Old me: *I did all that fantastic training, and have nothing to show for it.*
New me: *I didn't do the training to have "something to show for it." I know that I worked hard in my training. I had mono for most of last summer and it took a lot of patience, focus, and dedication to get back to my previous level of fitness, and even exceed it. This training cycle has given me the confidence to do even more with*

the next training cycle.

Old me: *My CAR teammates and friends are all setting PRs and improving. I am not.*
New me*: Some of these teammates and running friends haven't been running as long as I have, so they have more room for improvement relative to their natural ability. More importantly, thinking about other peoples' running is counterproductive. It will get me nowhere.*

I had become quite good at being able to identify the thoughts I *wanted* to have, but they weren't always automatic. Intellectually I was becoming an A+ student in sports psychology, but things still hadn't clicked for me emotionally. That was about to change.

* * *

Greg and I planned on running the 2013 Chicago Marathon in October. It was a race that had always been on my bucket list, and the big city atmosphere would provide a nice contrast to the smallness of B & A. I started to train for Chicago in June, but things came to an abrupt halt when I developed a stress reaction in my shin. I noticed the pain a few days before July 4th, which meant I wasn't able to run my traditional "Firecracker 5K" race.

This injury coincided with a new career opportunity. I enjoyed my marketing job at the educational software company, but a pre-IPO tech company found me on LinkedIn and invited me to interview there. My immediate response was no, primarily because the company was located in Arlington. Driving to Arlington during rush hour traffic would have taken over an hour each way and I didn't want to spend that kind of time commuting.

But after doing a bit of research, I learned that this company had a unique and fun culture and was listed as one of the best places to work in the Washington, D.C. metro area. The more I learned about the business, the more intrigued I became. Ultimately, the opportunity was too compelling to turn down, so I accepted their offer with a start date of July 8. I was so excited about this new tech company that the commute ended up not bothering me too much. I kept a positive attitude about it, and whenever traffic was really bad, I told myself that it was worth it. I couldn't control the traffic, but I could control how I handled it.

The CAR track workouts took place just two miles from my new office, and the office had its own gym with locker rooms. This meant that I could use the elliptical machine while recovering from the stress reaction in my shin, and once I was ready to run again, I could conveniently attend all of the group workouts.

My injury lingered for longer than expected. Initially, I thought I might be out for two weeks—definitely no more than three. But the pain didn't subside completely for six weeks. I maintained my fitness to the best of my ability by using the elliptical machine in my company's gym. One day, after completing a high-intensity elliptical workout I began to think about Chicago. As I was getting dressed for work in the locker room, I started to wonder if I'd be able to complete the marathon.

"Of course I'll be able to complete the marathon," I thought to myself. "It's just a matter of how long it will take me, given the impact of this injury. I might run a 4:00 marathon, but I still want to have the experience of Chicago. Other people may think I'm slow but …"

And then, BAM! It hit me. I saw the light. The walls came crumbing down.

"I can do whatever the hell I want!"

Even though I was alone in the locker room, I could feel a smile emerging on my face—a genuine smile. I felt this overwhelming and empowering sense of freedom.

I can do whatever the hell I want. What I wanted was to run the Chicago Marathon. I knew my time wouldn't be great because of the injury, but it didn't matter. I wanted to run Chicago, and I was going to run Chicago. It didn't matter what anyone else thought because it's what *I* wanted to do. This was my life and I finally felt like I was free to live it.

On the drive home that evening, I reflected more on my breakthrough:

I'm over it. Worrying about what other people think of me—I'm over it. Comparing my race times to others—I'm over that too. Obsessing over getting every run in and following a training plan perfectly—I'm over that. Exerting all of my mental energy around my next marathon—I'm done with it.

I'm basically just sick of all the crap that I put myself through. It serves no purpose; it's not going to make me a better runner. It's only going to undermine me and hurt me so why do I do it? It's okay that I took a month off of running. It's okay if I don't PR in Chicago. It's okay if I go for a year or two without setting a PR. Everything is my choice and nobody else cares about it to the extent that I do. Nobody is pressuring me to do any of these things except me. And I'm done with it.

* * *

I spent the first two weeks of August run-walking as my shin recovered from its stress reaction. It wasn't until the third week of August that I was able to resume somewhat normal training. A typical training cycle for me would have been twice as long, so I didn't have much time to build my long runs. Even so, I was able to squeeze in a 20-miler, two 16-milers, and a half marathon tune-up race.

I knew this wasn't an ideal marathon training cycle, and if my primary goal was to run a fast time, I could have bailed on Chicago and run the Richmond Marathon two months later. However, I was already registered for Chicago and I'd learned that running a satisfying marathon didn't have to mean setting a PR. I knew I would be able to train enough to get to the finish line, so I decided to go for it. I viewed Chicago as a fantastic opportunity to focus on goals other than a finish time, and still feel satisfied and accomplished.

During the week leading up to Chicago, I was as cool as a cucumber. I was hoping it was because my breakthrough was a true breakthrough, and it wasn't just because I had lower time expectations due to my injury. Ever since July, I had been sleeping phenomenally well. I hadn't experienced such peaceful sleep in over 10 years! Coming to the realization that I could do whatever I wanted to with my life and run whatever races I wanted to in whatever times I wanted was completely liberating. I felt like a new person.

Race morning arrived and Greg and I went through our standard routine. We both decided to carry water bottles and fill them up periodically throughout the race. I had revamped my nutrition and hydration plan in light of my digestive issues at B & A, and I was hopeful that my stomach would cooperate.

The weather was sunny and in the mid 50's. Even though many people thought that this was ideal weather, I wasn't a fan of the forecast. Earlier that year, I had bonked in a 10K when the conditions were 62 degrees and sunny. However, I ultimately knew there was nothing I could do about the weather, so I tried to think positively and not "expect" that the weather conditions would impact my race. No more self-fulfilling prophecies for me. I recapped the experience in my blog.

October 14, 2013

One of my goals was to soak it all up and enjoy the experience, and I made this my focus for these early miles. Instead of focusing on my pace and finish time, like I have in the past, I was focused on the race atmosphere, which relaxed me. The marathon is the only race distance in which I listen to music. It helps get me out of my head, and I find that good music can get me into a "zone" and enhance the adrenaline high. I carefully selected the songs and playlist order for this race, and I did the same for Greg. My plan was to start at around an 8:55 pace and speed up from there.

I settled into the race and my confidence began to build. I wasn't planning on speeding up all that much, but I just naturally started going faster and it felt great. The music contributed to my elevated mood. The band Panic! At The Disco *released a new CD on Tuesday, and so I put the entire thing on my playlist, starting at around mile 6. "Miss Jackson" is my favorite song from the CD, so I played it four times in a row, thinking this song is working for me, might as well just keep it going.*

This didn't really feel like a race to me. It felt like I was just running in a big city with a ton of other people, and with people all around me cheering. It was semi-surreal. I could hear the cheering, but I could also hear my music, so the whole thing just gave me this runner's high. Having fun? Check!

The next portion of the race was my favorite. It was at this point that I knew I wasn't going to have anxiety issues, and that the heat hadn't gotten to me (so far). I had imagined that the course wouldn't be shaded, but thankfully, about 3/4 of it was shaded. When I crossed the halfway mark in 1:55:06, I realized that I could probably run the second half faster and finish under 3:50. I wasn't sure by how much, but I told myself that the warm-up was over and now it was time to race a half marathon. I wanted to see how fast I could do it.

    I continued to execute my hydration and nutrition plan, drinking water about once a mile, and taking my SaltStick caps at the pre-determined times. During mile 15, I decided I would have one of the volunteers fill my water bottle from the big jug to make things go faster. Unfortunately, he was a very slow pourer, so I only had him fill it up 2/3 before moving on.

    I was excited because I knew the race was going to end well for me. At this point, I had all the confidence in the world that I would finish strong, as long as I remembered to keep pushing during those final miles. I had plenty of energy, the sun wasn't bothering me, and I was passing people like crazy. Passing other runners was fun, but also exhausting. I had to focus on where I was going to pass so as to not run into people. The race was still crowded, so I had to carefully maneuver around people. I easily passed the 3:50 pace group and felt excited to have done so. Usually when I see the 3:50 pace group, it's because I have hit the wall and they are passing me.

    I was in the home stretch! I noticed that my stomach felt really good, which is rare for this late in the game, and if I had brought another gel, I would have taken it. But since I packed the chews in anticipation of stomach distress, I had 4-5 of those instead. I started thinking about how happy I was to finally be running a solid marathon I kept on passing people, feeling strong. My quads started to hurt at around mile 20, but my energy level was high. I told myself to just deal with the quad pain and that it would be over soon.

    I finally ditched my water bottle during mile 24 and decided that if I needed more water I would drink from a cup. I really wanted the marathon to be over at this point and realized this was a sign that I was running an optimized race. You don't want it to feel easy at the end—it's supposed to hurt. I took this as a good sign and continued to push past people as I made my way to the finish.

I think that my Garmin read 26.2 miles at around 3:46, but due to so much back-and-forth weaving across the course, I hadn't run the most direct path from start to finish. The finish line was still far off in the distance. As I approached it, I noticed that I would be on the border of 3:47 and 3:48. I wanted that 3:47 so badly! This is where looking at the Garmin can be motivating. I gave it everything I had at the very end, but there was a surprise hill just before the finish line, so it wasn't fast enough to get my 3:47. According to the official race results, I ran the first half in 1:55:06 and the second half in 1:53:04, yielding a time of 3:48:10.

Chicago was a very good race for me on many levels. I would even consider it a landmark race, since I haven't run this well since 2008, and I have run 8 marathons since then (not to mention the 3 I started but did not finish). The most important aspect of this marathon was that I went into it with the right attitude. I knew that I wasn't in as good a shape as I had been for most of my previous marathons, and yet I still had the confidence that focusing on "the process" of running would yield a favorable outcome. I didn't speculate as to what my time would be, and time wasn't really the focus here. It's a valuable lesson because the next time I run a marathon with a solid training cycle under my belt, I will know that the feeling of accomplishment can come from so many areas other than a time. And I won't think that my training was wasted if something goes wrong and I don't do well.

While it may seem that I lowered my expectations for this race, I actually raised them. I was focused on areas that were traditionally a challenge for me and I truly embraced the process. I "expected" that I wasn't going to come down hard on myself, and I was determined to make Chicago a great experience for myself no matter what. I started this race conservatively, and didn't force myself into a narrow window of finish times that I had to hit. I went into the race with the attitude that I would try my best, stick to my plan, and enjoy the ride. And in the process of doing all of that, I just happened to run my strongest marathon in five years, setting a PR of 40 seconds. And unofficially, according to my Garmin, I set a 26.2-mile PR of about three minutes.

Once I changed my mindset about my expectations, the rest was easy. Sleep was easy. Having fun was easy. Enjoying the entire weekend with Greg was easy. And yet this was major progress for me, so I consider them huge wins. I couldn't have asked for a better experience, and I have a renewed love of marathon running.

CHAPTER 15:
TRYING EASY

November 1, 2015

Coach Greg McMillan says that sometimes you need to "try easier"—let it flow, have fun and release the reins when "trying harder" isn't getting you to your goal.

I'm now halfway between my two goal races for the fall season: the Columbus Half Marathon and the Richmond Half Marathon. I've never been able to run as fast as I can now, and sometimes I'm amazed at the paces I log during my workouts— they keep dropping. I think I've learned to simply "try easier" and let the fitness come to me, instead of chasing it.

For the first time in nearly 10 years, I've made a conscious decision to not run a fall marathon. Instead, I'm working on tackling different challenges: the half marathon and of course, writing this book. I'm focusing just as much on recovering from hard workouts as I am actually doing the workouts. Looking back on my blog from years ago, I would use one key workout or one peak training week as proof that I was getting faster. Now, I am looking more at consistency and the big picture of my runs. By releasing the so-called "reins," I've finally gotten to a fitness level that I always dreamt about attaining. It almost feels like it was too easy to get here, now that I've let go of all the unnecessary junk getting in my way.

* * *

Three weeks after the Chicago Marathon, I ran the New York City Marathon. The opportunity to run NYC arose prior to Chicago. Through various connections, I received a VIP entry into the race from Asics, the race sponsor, free of charge. Even though I had previously determined that I wouldn't run the NYC Marathon again, I couldn't turn down a free VIP entry that included special transportation to the start line, exclusive start line amenities, and hundreds of dollars' worth of free NYC Marathon gear. It was actually one of my good friends who had "connections," so the two of us both ran this race.

Having just run the Chicago Marathon three weeks prior, I was planning to simply run NYC at my easy pace and enjoy the experience. I did this, but ended up with major digestive issues during the eighth mile, and pulled off the course into several different restaurants for multiple bathroom stops. Instead of letting this setback get me down and ruin the rest of my race, I remained optimistic and was able to turn things around. I also used this race to practice some of the mental toughness tools that Neal had taught me.

November 4, 2013

I'm glad I took advantage of this opportunity. I ran the race to the best of my ability, kept positive even when my stomach was acting up, and focused on the experience rather than the time on the clock. I ran the second half only 2 minutes slower than the first half, which shows that despite all of the stomach drama and leg stuff at the end, I was overall pretty consistent with my pacing.

Because I was injured for six weeks this past summer, this fall season has been a great opportunity to focus on the mental aspect of racing—the area where I struggle most. Now that I have two "positive" marathon experiences under my belt, I am beginning to see the marathon as something to enjoy, and not something where I have to go out and prove to the world that I am a great runner. Of course I will ultimately want to run faster and set PRs, but in order to do that, I first needed to establish that it's not just about the finish time. Marathoning can offer a great deal of personal satisfaction even if the time on the clock isn't as fast as I would like, or as fast as I think it "should" be based on training. It's taken me 16 marathons to figure this out, but I'm glad I finally did.

This fall racing season has set me up to continue marathoning in a much more positive light than ever before, and I look forward to being able to train consistently and tie the whole package together at some point!

* * *

It was an exceptionally cold winter. Temperatures were in the single digits on a regular basis in the mornings when I ran. I tried to avoid the treadmill as much as possible, but with ice on the ground and a "real-feel" of below zero degrees, there were days when I had no other option.

I was more focused on my career than I ever had been previously. I'd never had such a challenging job where the bar was set so high, and I loved it. I managed a relatively large team and was able to make a substantial impact on the company's success. I decided to wait until late spring to run another marathon because I needed to focus as much mental energy as possible on work during January and February. I was responsible for spearheading the company's first-ever client conference, which was scheduled for late February in Miami Beach. It was a high-pressure environment and the company was investing a great deal of time and resources, and it ultimately all fell on me to make sure the event was successful.

It was the first time since I started running marathons that I dedicated more mental energy to my job than to my running. It was a combination of having an extremely demanding job, and also being able to free up some mental space for other things. The danger, of course, was not to begin to define myself by my career achievements. I definitely did not want to pass my perfectionistic nature from an eating disorder to marathon running to a career obsession. I was learning to become a more balanced person overall, and not have any one area of my life define me.

The conference was a huge success, and even though I didn't always enjoy managing all the tiny details, I experienced a great deal of satisfaction when the event turned out so well. I was actually able to run while I was in Miami, and I even led an organized group run for our conference attendees. I had the opportunity to run alongside our CEO as well as executives at large utility companies from all over the world. It was definitely an interesting merger of my running career and my marketing career.

The challenge with running a late spring marathon was the potential for warm weather. Based on my previous experiences at Shamrock, I knew that even March races could be warm, so Greg and I decided to travel north. I had heard great things about the Mississauga Marathon from one of my Canadian friends, so we registered for it.

I ran two tune-up races in preparation: the Shamrock Half Marathon (yes, I was going back there) and the Cherry Blossom Ten Miler. The Shamrock Half Marathon did not go as well as I had hoped, and I struggled to not revert back to my former self. I faced a brutal headwind for several miles in the middle of the race, and I let it discourage me. After having lost at least a minute during that portion of the race, I felt defeated and had a negative attitude for the rest of the race.

Similar to the Richmond Half Marathon in 2012, many of my friends set PRs in the half marathon, and I was the only one still stuck in the 1:40's. Even though I knew that comparing myself to other people wasn't a good idea, I could not shake the feeling that everyone else was progressing with their running and I had hit a plateau. I had hoped to break 1:40, but ended up running a 1:42:24. I was disappointed both with my time and how I handled my feelings. I wished that I had been mentally tougher during the windy portion of the race, and it felt like nobody else's time suffered to the extent that mine did because of the wind.

Ultimately, I knew I needed to turn this race into a learning experience, so that I could know what *not* to do in future races:

March 30, 2014

I've heard the phrase "pushing past limits" over and over again throughout my running career. Whether it comes up in the blogs I read, on Facebook posts, in running magazines or during in-person conversations with other runners, it's a very common theme. I've never given the phrase much thought and honestly, it's always seemed to be a cliché. But now I am starting to really think about what it means to push beyond one's limits.

I'm at the stage in my running where PRs will be few and far between. I've run 100+ races over the course of 8 years, with over 10,000 training miles, and I'm starting to question if I am at my peak or if I still have the potential to run faster. Greg pointed out that it's only within the past year that I have truly addressed my mental barriers, and I'm finally starting to arrive at races well rested and relaxed. Mental limits can be the most difficult to identify and break through, and I think I am making great strides there.

I think my next challenge will be pushing past my pain tolerance during races. I always think I push myself as hard as possible, because racing always hurts so much; but then I wonder if there is a certain amount of pain that is familiar to me during races, and if I push past that, I would fear blowing up and not being able to sustain it. And therefore, I am afraid to run past a certain pain threshold. I think most runners (well, I guess all runners) have this threshold, but I think I can push mine further. One of my goals for my next few races will be to push past my pain tolerance without the fear of a blow-up. I want to truly trust my training and realize that my limiting factor is my mind, not my body.

When I ran the Cherry Blossom 10-miler a few weeks later, I vowed that I would push really, really hard and not let something like the wind get in my way. I told myself that I would be mentally prepared to fight and stay strong.

The result was that I shaved 25 seconds off of my 10-mile PR. I was pleased with the outcome, but it also opened my eyes to the fact that I might be plateauing physically. I knew that I hadn't run a marathon to my full physical potential yet, but I've run other distances to my full potential, particularly the Cherry Blossom 10-miler.

I decided that I would look into a new training approach after Mississauga, no matter how the race went. After all, I'd been following the same plan for the past several years, and I was getting bored with it. My average weekly mileage was usually in the 50's. I ran intervals every Tuesday (and those workouts didn't vary much), and tempo runs each Thursday, anywhere from 3-6 miles. I suspected that lack of variation in my training was preventing me from making more substantial fitness gains.

The Mississauga Marathon arrived, and my primary goal for the race was to build on the mindset I had during the Cherry Blossom 10-miler: continue to push hard when things get tough; expect for the race to be difficult; have a plan for staying mentally positive and pushing through tough times; be confident in knowing that I will be able to deal with whatever the race throws at me. I focused heavily on this goal during the two weeks leading up to the marathon.

I wasn't hung up on a particular time goal, although I had a range of times that I thought was realistic, given my fitness level. As a result, I slept better than I ever had in the week leading up to the race. I had very little, if any, anxiety about Mississauga. And that's because I felt completely in control. When I had previously focused so much on my goal time, it would stress me out because I didn't know if I would get it. I had a huge fear of the unknown. But by focusing on what I could control—my mental will to stay strong—I remained as cool as a cucumber. Before the race ever began I felt like I had achieved so much:

- The taper didn't feel like something to "survive"—it was just a normal two weeks.
- My sleep was restful and I got enough of it.
- I was injury free: I had felt a hip injury coming on in mid-March, which I staved off through strengthening exercises and religious foam rolling.

I had also come to terms with Boston. A few days before the race, I realized that I wanted to run Boston, but it didn't define who I was as a runner or a person. It was just something I wanted to do eventually, and the fact that I hadn't done it yet didn't make me any less of a runner. I no longer saw it as a goal or a dream of mine. But it was also not something that I was trying to ignore or avoid. Boston was simply a marathon with a qualifying standard, and I planned on running it eventually.

May 5, 2014

Every day I sit in traffic for 45-60 minutes, and I never get angry or frustrated or annoyed by the traffic. I expect it, accept it, and deal with it. I rarely arrive home in a bad mood because of it. I signed up for this traffic when I took this new job last July, and so I have ways of coping with it in order to stay relaxed. Similarly, when I sign up for a marathon, or any race for that matter, I should expect that it will be hard and it will hurt. And sometimes it will be a lot harder than I think it "should" be. Regardless, I need to accept it and know exactly how I will deal with it when it happens. I'm not somebody who gets angry at traffic during my commute. And I'm not somebody who gets discouraged when a race throws a curve ball.

At the Mississauga Marathon yesterday, I was prepared for whatever the race would bring. It was 41 degrees and windy. I knew the wind would be a factor in the race, but I was hopeful that it would primarily be a tailwind. The wind was out of the WNW, and the course was a net east, but there was a lot of back-and-forth running and turns along the way that I was mentally preparing for.

My plan was to run the first half in around 1:50-1:51 and the second half in 1:48 or faster. I planned to run the first six miles at a pace of around 8:30-8:35 and then speed up. I had enjoyed a two-minute negative split in Chicago and felt great at the end, so I figured I would try the same approach here. My time goal range was 3:35-3:45. The race was actually measured in kilometers— 42.2K. It was pretty cool to have kilometer markers instead of mile markers because there were more of them. However, I paced the race based on miles, and I had my Garmin to tell me what mile I was on so that I could execute a pacing strategy that I was familiar with.

I spent the early miles taking in the scenery, relaxing, and just enjoying the race. I noticed the wind, but the course was relatively sheltered at this point, and the winds weren't as strong as they would be later in the race. The Mississauga course advertises itself as a net downhill course, which is true, but very deceiving. The net downhill occurs within the first 10 miles and then the rest of the race is rolling hills.

Mile: 1: 8:35
Mile 2: 8:32
Mile 3: 8:16
Mile 4: 8:32
Mile 5: 8:31
Mile 6: 8:20

The half marathon runners turned off at around mile 8, and the crowd thinned out. Mile 7 featured a long hill, which I wasn't expecting. That would be the first of many hills that you don't really see when looking at the course elevation profile. I think my reluctance to push up hills in the past was due to my fear that I would expend too much effort and then blow up. But during this race, I had a great deal of confidence and my goal was to push through the hard stuff—which meant toughing it out on the hills.

Most mistakes in the marathon are made within the first 10K, and I felt like I had done a great job of being conservative early on. I ditched my throwaway arm warmers and gloves as the sun rose and the temperatures climbed into the upper 40's. We ran through some residential areas with beautiful houses, and I found myself really relishing the experience—waving to people, smiling, and just feeling a huge sense of happiness.

Mile 7: 8:48
Mile 8: 8:12
Mile 9: 8:19
Mile 10: 8:42
Mile 11: 8:31
Mile 12: 8:26
Mile 13: 8:15

I felt amazing during miles 14-17. I saw people holding Boston signs and I thought to myself, "I'm going to Boston!" and this huge feeling of excitement swept over me. Everything was great. No stomach issues. No anxiety issues. My legs felt strong. Everything felt wonderful. Okay, yes, there was a tailwind and a downhill, but to feel so great at mile 17 of a marathon was awesome!

During these three miles, I noticed two runners with marathon bibs running on a path alongside the road in the opposite direction. I wondered if they dropped out and why they were running the course backwards. And then I saw more runners on that path. And then it hit me—pretty soon, this nice downhill/tailwind combo would turn into an uphill/headwind combo. That was a scary thought. I put it out of my mind and told myself I would deal with it when I encountered it.

I saw Greg at around mile 16 as he was on his way back and I was wondering how he was coping with going in the other direction. At the turnaround there was a sign that said something like, "Sorry! Just a little out and back." That sign made me smile. I turned around and things started out okay, but it wasn't long before the 20 mph headwinds came. I tried drafting off of other runners, but I found that I wanted to run faster than the people I could draft off of. I kept passing people instead of drafting. Finally, there was a guy in a bright orange windbreaker whom I was able to draft off of. Unfortunately, it didn't really work. I didn't feel any relief from the wind by being behind him and his windbreaker.

Mile 18 was when I started to really push. Unlike with past marathons, I had no thoughts of "this sucks" or "this is unfair" or "this is so hard" or "there goes my sub-3:40." I didn't think about it. I just ran through it. I didn't even need to tell myself anything mentally. I just kept listening to my music and kept running. My mind was pretty quiet as I just pushed through the wind and up the long hill, passing people one by one. Finally, at mile 19, we turned around and I let out a huge sigh of relief. Orange windbreaker guy looked back at me and I smiled.

Mile 14: 8:13
Mile 15: 8:16
Mile 16: 8:22
Mile 17: 8:16
Mile 18: 8:47 (20 mph headwind)
Mile 19: 8:24
Mile 20: 8:38

There were many turns and hills during these final miles, which

*made the course more challenging. Greg later told me that he liked
the variation of so many turns and weaving through the area, but
for me it was mentally draining to have to change direction and to
go from road to path back to road and then path. We ran down by
the water, which was beautiful, but only for about 5 minutes at a
time before we were routed away from the water and back onto the
streets. Because of the continued back and forth, there were a lot
of hills that I wasn't anticipating. And it also meant that we spent a
lot of time running into the 22 mph headwind.*

*Many people were struggling. I passed people who were
walking up the hills and people who were doing the survival
shuffle. Orange windbreaker guy stayed strong and I kept him in
my sights at all times. I glanced down at my Garmin and saw that I
had an 8:29 pace average for the race. I was hurting pretty badly
and the wind was really taking it out of me, but I did not want that
number to slip too much. I had gotten this far with it, and I was
going to do whatever it took to hang on. I took my last gel at mile
21 and then ditched my water bottle. It felt great to not have that in
my hands anymore as I used my arms to push up hills and against
the wind.*

*The last three miles were so mentally exhausting because of
all the curves and turns. I just wanted to zone out and run in a
straight line. I didn't like not knowing where I would be going. But
never did a negative thought enter my mind. I just kept pushing. I
was definitely hurting and worn out, but I was going to give 100%
and have no regrets.*

*Even with 0.2 miles to go, I still couldn't see the finish line!
But I gunned it anyway, running the last 0.2 miles at a 7:46 pace.
They called my name right before I crossed the finish line and it
felt amazing!!!*

*Mile 21: 8:24
Mile 22: 9:10
Mile 23: 8:35
Mile 24: 9:14
Mile 25: 8:44
Mile 26: 8:53*

I finished in 3:43:44, which is a PR by over 4 minutes! This was a much more challenging course than I expected. I thought it was going to be flat during the second half, but instead it was hilly. I didn't think the 22 mph winds would be headwinds for as much of the race as they were, but I pushed through. I am super proud of myself for hanging in there, never having negative thoughts and just pushing all the way through to the end. That's what this sport is all about.

I didn't qualify for Boston, which means I will have to wait until 2016 at the earliest, but I am totally cool with that. And hey—if this were two years ago before they changed the qualifying standards, it would be a BQ. My major takeaway is that I am finally at a place with my marathoning where I am feeling confident and relaxed going into the races, and not afraid to face obstacles.

PART VI

A BEGINNING

CHAPTER 16:
THE OTHER SIDE

November 21, 2015

I've always seen the Boston Marathon as the endgame—a victory lap. Another accomplishment to check off of my list. A rite of passage into the world of "fast" runners. In my mind, there were the "haves" and the "have-nots" of marathon runners, and I had always fallen into the have-not club. I thought that qualifying for Boston would fundamentally change my identity as a person, and I never gave much thought to what would come next.

Qualifying for the Boston Marathon is not an entitlement. It's not even something that can be earned by following a training plan and reaching a particular level of physical fitness. The only way to qualify for Boston is to execute on race day. The notion that I "deserved" Boston was a huge flaw in my thinking for years, and it would leave me feeling robbed or cheated whenever a marathon didn't go my way. There are so many factors that come into play, many of which are controllable, and many of which are not.

The ability to identify what I can and cannot control combined with a separation of my core identity from my running has freed me from the shackles that held me back for so many years. The application of this seemingly simple skill to my daily life, in everything that I do, has allowed me an overall sense of wellbeing. It's somewhat ironic that only in the absence of obsession can I truly accomplish the things that I would otherwise obsess about.

Boston is now a reality, and I plan to approach it the same way that I've approached all of my races this year: boldly, without fear of failure, and with high expectations of pushing the boundaries. It's not an endgame—it's the beginning of a new chapter.

* * *

Even though I was pleased with my Mississauga performance, I felt like I had hit a physical plateau. I was also getting bored with my training plan. The idea of doing the same tempo runs and intervals week after week didn't seem exciting and I wanted to change things up. I figured it was time to invest in a personal coach—one who would provide me with a plan tailored to my specific needs. Even though I enjoyed the team atmosphere of the Capital Area Runners, there was little variation and no personalization.

I knew that the McMillan Running Company, the creators of my favorite running calculator, offered personal coaching. I looked into it further and it sounded like it would be a great fit for me. I completed an extensive questionnaire about my running history and goals. I told them that I had been racing for about 10 years, and that I was looking to break through a plateau. I provided a link to my online training log so that they could see the specifics of my training, as well as a history of my running-related injuries. They paired me with Coach Andrew Lemoncello, The McMillan Running Company's resident Olympian, whose resume was extremely impressive.

Having a personal coach and a training plan tailored specifically to my needs was re-energizing. Doing new workouts and trying a different approach brought new life into my training, and I found myself excited to tackle new challenges. There were some key differences between Coach Andrew's plan and how I had been training previously:

- Most of the runs were time-based instead of distance-based (e.g., "run 60 minutes" instead of "run 6 miles").
- The plan had no weekly mileage "targets" to hit unless I estimated how much distance I would run in the allotted timeframe.
- I only received four weeks of training at a time, forcing me to trust that my coach had a long-term plan in mind, and keeping me focused on the present.
- There was a great deal of variation from week to week. Workouts were very rarely repeated.
- There was more of a focus on shorter intervals.
- The long runs didn't get all that long until 8-10 weeks pre-marathon.

Prior to working with Coach Andrew, I had never run an interval shorter than 400 meters. Andrew's plan incorporated very short time-based intervals, as short as 15 seconds. I realized that even if I didn't get any faster, I was enjoying running so much more. Each workout was a new challenge, and some of them looked quite intimidating on paper. This allowed for a huge sense of satisfaction upon successfully completing the workouts.

The plan also violated some of the "rules" that I had previously instituted for myself. For example, I had a rule that I would never run the day after a race—I would use that day to recover. Coach Andrew scheduled long runs the day after 5K races. He even scheduled a 60-minute run the day after a half marathon. But I trusted him, and lo and behold—I was able to do everything on the program without getting injured. Working with Coach Andrew taught me to challenge my preconceived notions about training and break through boundaries that I had arbitrarily imposed on myself.

I was still working with Neal, but at this point I was only seeing him once every 3-4 weeks. We agreed that I had come to a much healthier spot, and that weekly visits were no longer necessary. However, there was still plenty to work on in terms of mental toughness *during* a race, and also in other areas of my life.

My next target race was the Columbus Marathon in October. I had heard great things about the course and organization from one of my CAR friends, and Columbus was relatively easy to travel to. It was a large race, but not nearly as massive as Chicago or New York City.

Four weeks before Columbus, I ran the Rock 'n' Roll Philadelphia Half Marathon as a tune-up race. It was definitely a test of the mental skills that I had learned from Neal. And even though the race objectively did not go well, I was still able to feel satisfied and accomplished. It was an unseasonably warm and humid morning for late September in Philadelphia. I knew that the conditions were far from ideal, but I didn't let this upset me or worry me. I had fully accepted that the weather was not within my control, so my job was to simply run to the best of my ability. I decided that I would run based on perceived effort level, instead of trying to hit certain paces.

I knew that I didn't fare as well as other runners in the heat and humidity. Neal had always challenged this belief, and suggested that perhaps it was a self-fulfilling prophecy. I refused to believe that this was all in my head—I had too much evidence that showed that I simply wasn't as competitive as I was in cooler conditions. However, I was open to the possibility that I was making it worse by obsessing over it. I was determined to run my best race possible. Realistically, I knew that I would run slower than if the weather were cooler, but I wasn't upset or pouty about it, like I had been in so many previous races.

I began the race at a pace of 7:45 and was able to maintain it for about six miles. At that point, I began to struggle. When I came to the 8-mile marker, I looked down at the split on my Garmin and my pace was well into the 8's. I was surprised. I didn't feel like I had slowed down that much, and I was exerting a greater level of effort than I had been at the beginning of the race.

I asked myself if I was truly giving 100% and the answer was yes. I told myself that my goal was to run a race that I would be proud of. I needed to make sure that I was always giving 100% at all times and never giving up. No matter how badly I felt, no matter what the watch said, I was going to give 100%.

I energized myself, I motivated myself, and I told myself I could do it. Unfortunately, reality kicked in shortly thereafter and I found myself struggling. At that point, I was doing everything in my power to maintain my effort and not give up. Physically, I just couldn't go any faster.

I crossed the finish line and I saw Greg. At first, I was not able to talk to him. I tried to get words out, but they wouldn't come. Then, I started to feel disoriented. I started having strange thoughts, like the thoughts I have when I am starting to fall asleep and dream. I panicked because I thought I was going to pass out, which made things worse. But ultimately, I was okay. I just needed a while to recover. My official time was 1:47:14.

In the past, I would have felt robbed, frustrated, angry, and depressed. But instead, I truly felt satisfied. I pushed through a difficult race and maintained a positive attitude the entire time. That was huge progress.

September 22, 2014

Although this is one of my slowest half marathons in the past five years, I feel good about my performance. While I know I'm not supposed to compare myself to others, I think this race confirms what I have suspected for years—the heat and humidity affect me more than the average runner. I think that most runners probably ran a good 2-4 minutes slower than they would have in cooler, less humid weather. For me, that delta is more like 6-8 minutes. I trained all summer in the humid weather. And I actually ran pretty well in the humidity during training. But when I am putting out 100% effort, my body doesn't respond well.

It's nothing to be upset about, but rather something to simply accept. Training in the heat and humidity will help me acclimate, but it will only go so far. The good thing about this race was that I didn't go into it "expecting" to bonk. I went into it with confidence and I ran it by feel. Unfortunately, my body wasn't able to sustain a fast pace under those conditions. So, what are the key takeaways from this race?

- *I've come a long way in terms of reducing my race anxiety and being able to sleep in the days leading up to the race.*
- *I used positive self-talk to get myself through the tough parts, and I made sure that I was always running my best, no matter how crappy I felt or how slow the pace.*

- *I know that the heat/humidity is not "all in my head" and that I truly am affected by these conditions to a greater extent than most people—even if I train in these conditions and am well acclimated.*
- *I know I have the mental toughness I need to get through the marathon in a few weeks.*

All in all, this was not the race I hoped for, but it is a race I am proud of.

* * *

I went into the Columbus Marathon feeling relaxed, confident, and well prepared. I had somewhat of an achy left hip, but it wasn't something that I thought would hinder my performance. It was a sunny day, with temperatures in the low 40's and light winds. My plan was to start at a pace of 8:20, and then speed up slightly to run a half marathon of around 1:49:00. Then, I wanted to negative split, resulting in a time of around 3:35 (give or take 2 minutes in either direction). I was in new territory with my fitness level and relaxed mental state, so I had no idea what I was capable of.

October 19, 2014

I ran with Greg for the first mile and then turned my headphones on after he ran ahead. It was crowded. I think this race has over 15,000 participants if you include all the half marathoners. I knew that with so many people blocking my view, running the tangents would be impossible for the first half.

My hip started to hurt during mile 5. Instead of worrying, I told myself, "Think of it this way, you don't have a bad hip—you have one good hip!" I stayed relaxed during these early miles and everything felt great, as it tends to do at the beginning of a marathon. I was really focused on my music during these miles, and that definitely helped me relax.

Mile 1: 8:41
Mile 2: 8:34

Mile 3: 8:14
Mile 4: 8:16
Mile 5: 8:10
Mile 6: 8:08
Mile 7: 8:23

I was cruising for miles 8-13. I ran slightly faster than planned, but it was mainly downhill, so it felt manageable. I also realized that my Garmin was beeping well before the mile markers. I was doing a miserable job at running the most direct path simply because I couldn't see when the turns and curves were coming up. This meant that my Garmin pace would be faster than my official race pace. I knew this wasn't something I should be focusing on, so I quickly got that thought out of my head. I reached the halfway point at 1:48:46, which was almost exactly what I had planned. It gave me a huge confidence boost that I was executing well.

Mile 8: 8:12
Mile 9: 8:05
Mile 10: 8:08
Mile 11: 8:23
Mile 12: 8:17
Mile 13: 8:06
Mile 14: 8:08

I knew that the next portion would be the toughest part of the course and I was mentally prepared. Miles 17-19 are a net uphill, and there were some pretty large ones in there. I kept telling myself it was going to get better, and not to worry if I slowed down a little bit. I knew that a downhill section would be coming once I reached mile 19. At mile 18, I ditched my hand-held water bottle even though I still needed it to take one more gel. It was too exhausting to carry it and I needed to be pumping my arms on the hills. These hills were not as steep or as long as they were in Mississauga, but for whatever reason, they hurt a lot more. And my left hip was on fire.

Mile 15: 8:14
Mile 16: 8:15

Mile 17: 8:16
Mile 18: 8:40
Mile 19: 8:41
Mile 20: 8:20

The final miles were advertised as the fastest of the course, and my coach had told me that this is where he wanted me to speed up and hammer it home. Well, I ended up being happy to simply hang on to a decent pace rather than speeding up. My original plan was to run these last miles at an 8:10 pace, but that wasn't happening. Aside from my hip (which was killing me at this point), my legs felt strong and not as tired as they normally are at this point in the race. The limiting factor was my energy level and overall feeling of fatigue.

I think the problem in these last miles was my lack of nutrition and hydration. I had one more gel that I planned to take at mile 22, and I had to stop at a water station to do so since my bottle was gone. When I did that, my reflex was to spit out the gel just as quickly as I squeezed it in my mouth. And then I tried having some water, and I spit that out as well. I pushed forward. I felt like death, and every time I started to question why I put myself through this torture, I immediately replaced those thoughts with "you can do it" and "stay strong."

Mile 21: 8:22
Mile 22: 8:18
Mile 23: 8:25
Mile 24: 8:38
Mile 25: 8:24

During the last mile, I started thinking about my finish time as motivation. I told myself that I had to speed up if I wanted to qualify for Boston. I thought about all of the years of hard work I had put into this—all the tears and disappointments. Over 10,000 training miles logged. This was it. All I had to do was run fast for another mile and a half. I channeled all of my resources and it wasn't until just before the mile-26 marker that the adrenaline truly set in.

When my Garmin showed 26.2 miles, the total time was 3:37:xx. However, due to not running the tangents, the finish line was still a few hundred meters away. Dammit! I wanted that BQ! Somewhere deep within me, I found a hidden gear and I bolted for the finish line at pace of 7:21. Previously, I hadn't even been able to maintain an 8:21 pace. My desire for this BQ was so great that I tore through the last 0.2 mile, passing everyone in my sight. I could literally see my BQ potential slipping away by the second. But I wouldn't let it happen. It would not get away from me.

I crossed the finish line and stopped my watch. I looked down, and it read 3:40:01. I had no idea if I had gotten that elusive BQ or not! It was possible that my official time was a 3:40:00, which was a BQ. On the flip side, I could have missed it by a mere second! The suspense was killing me, and so was my hip.

As it turns out, I did qualify for Boston. With a 3:40:00. Not a single second to spare. I think it suits me. It's kind of funny, and kind of appropriate. In the grand scheme of things, the Boston qualifying journey has been about so much more than running. It's been about perseverance, dedication, mental strength and most importantly, learning how to truly accept my imperfect self. I would not be the person I am today if I had qualified back in 2008.

The reality is that a 3:40:00 will likely not get me a spot in the 2016 Boston Marathon. Because the race doesn't have enough spots for all of its qualifiers, the new registration process only accepts the fastest of those who have met the official qualifying standards. As much as I want to run Boston, I don't feel like this diminishes the achievement in any way. I will try to get my time down next spring, but Columbus was my first official Boston qualifying finish. It's mine. The fact that it was the slowest possible BQ I could have possibly gotten is kind of special. And now that I've done it, I will have the confidence to do it again.

Even though I didn't hit my goal time, I still feel truly accomplished and I'm ready to train even harder for the next one. Boston I qualified for, and Boston I shall run.

CHAPTER 17:
THE PAYOFF

My commitment to overcoming perfectionism has been the best thing I've ever done for myself. Instead of waking up on edge each morning without feeling truly relaxed, I gradually emerge from sleep with a stillness that seems foreign. After having spent the majority of my adult life shackled by anxiety, depression, and insomnia, I now feel free. I *am* a good person, doing both good and great things.

One of the greatest challenges of the marathon is accepting that an extraordinary amount of hard work and preparation seems to all boil down to something that happens within just a few hours. It can feel devastating when such a large investment of time and effort doesn't pay off—particularly when it happens repeatedly. Looking for that payoff where I *know* I can find it has been the key to unlocking my mental handcuffs.

I get paid almost every day. How? Because marathon training is a daily commitment to being my best self, both physically and mentally, and there's an immense amount of personal satisfaction to be found in that. Life is too short to feel like I'm wasting months (or even years) of my time on something that may or may not turn out the way I want it to. I don't sweat the small stuff, but I also look to the small stuff to find fulfillment on a daily basis.

* * *

"I don't like loud music playing on the course when I'm running," I said to Neal shortly after the Columbus Marathon.

"What do you mean you don't like it?" He asked.

"It's jarring and distracts my focus," I replied.

"So, are you going to let loud music influence your performance?"

"No, it's just annoying."

"Then why even bother to pay attention? Why even have that thought go through your mind?"

Neal proceeded to tell me that what I like and don't like in a race atmosphere is irrelevant. He pointed out that I was extremely sensitive and that I had opinions on almost everything in a race: was it too crowded, too windy, too loud, too hilly, too unorganized, and so on. He told me that the most successful athletes ignore the things they don't like. They assess whether or not they need to adjust something based on a circumstance, and if not, then they simply ignore it. Essentially I was wasting mental energy on things that I couldn't control.

I let his point sink in and I realized how much sense it made. And then I thought about all the times I ran races where I acknowledged things I simply didn't like. As I proved to myself during the Love Rox Half Marathon, I was past the point of letting those things discourage me, but why was I still wasting mental energy even making those kinds of judgments?

"Instead of thinking to yourself that you don't like the music," Neal said, "why not simply ignore it? Or if you if can't ignore it then think to yourself, 'Yep, there's music.'"

I had the opportunity to practice this skill and several others during a 15K race in January. The Frostbite 15K in Richmond was on my schedule as a tune-up race for the B & A Trail Marathon. I had decided to return to B & A in March for my next marathon for the same reasons I had run it the first time—I enjoyed the low-key atmosphere and the easy logistics.

The Frostbite 15K was reminiscent of the New Jersey Marathon from 2009—a cold, wet downpour. With temperatures in the high 30's and rain coming down in buckets, it definitely was not an ideal day for a race. I actually came close to bailing on this race completely. I had heard that there was a section of the course that was flooded to the extent that even cars couldn't pass. I thought it might be better to drive back home, wait for the rain to stop and the temperatures to rise and do a long run. Five minutes before the start of the race, I was still debating whether or not to run the race. Ultimately, though, I decided that it would be the perfect test of my mental toughness, so I embraced it instead of shying away from it.

In terms of goals, my original goals had been to see what I could do at a new distance, stay strong on the hills, and run around a 7:20 pace. However, once I realized that the course would be slippery and there could be some obstacles, I determined that my main goal was just to stick it out and maintain a strong effort.

January 18, 2015

As I began the race, my spirits were so-so. I had only warmed up for five minutes, which wasn't ideal, and there were huge puddles everywhere. I was cold right from the start. Even still, I was running pretty fast and my 7:25 pace felt more like a 7:40 pace, which was awesome. The early miles were uneventful, but I decided I would stick with it and run the best race I could, given the conditions. The rain was coming down in buckets, and I was completely soaked after one mile.

Another challenge that I quickly realized was how curvy the course was. I had been warned about this, and had planned on running the tangents, but with so many puddles and with the road being slanted and uneven, I spent my energy watching my footing instead of running tangents.

Things started to get dicey 4 miles into the race and I had to put on the brakes. Usually I run down hills pretty quickly, but I was afraid to go all out on this course due to how slippery it was. My top priority was to finish the race safely, and if that meant spending more energy on watching my footing and being careful, then that's what I would do. I reached the flooded area during mile 5 and we were diverted onto the grass/mud. I slowed to my "easy" pace during this short portion because it was slippery and muddy and difficult to run on. But after that, my spirits lifted and I got back into race mode.

At some point during mile 7 the rain really picked up, and so did the wind. It was a complete downpour and I was freezing. I had memories of the New Jersey marathon from 2009 when I was taken to the medical tent afterwards for hypothermia. My motivation was to finish quickly, without hypothermia and to get warm as soon as possible. Usually during a race I want the race to be over because I'm pushing so hard and I just don't want to be exerting that kind of effort. Here, my effort level was admittedly not race effort, and all I wanted to do was get out of the rain. Part of me was worried that if I went all out, I'd get sick and put too much a strain on my body in that kind of weather. And part of me was still holding back due to the slippery roads and uneven pavement.

Given how horrible I felt, my spirits remained relatively high. During the Love Rox Half Marathon back in 2013, I was angry and unhappy. During this race, I was "neutral" about the weather and focused on just getting to the finish line and putting out a hard effort.

Finally, I reached the finish line. I went inside the school to check out the results, but there was no way I was sticking around for a potential award. I needed to get out of those soaking clothes ASAP. Thankfully, one of my good friends lives less than a mile away from this school and I was able to shower at her place.

My time was 1:12:10. My "official" race pace is probably a lot slower than my Garmin pace, due to the course being 9.5 miles. It wasn't a long course, but there was no way to run the tangents and it was extremely curvy. My Garmin pace for the race was 7:37, which I think is pretty good given how hilly and slippery this course was.

Although this race was intended to be a tune-up and "check-in" on my fitness level, it ended up being more about taking "what the day gives you" and toughing it out. I put out a solid effort, kept a positive attitude, didn't bail on the race, and placed 2nd in my age group. I didn't focus on the fact that the weather sucked. I focused on making sure that I didn't slip and fall while pushing my way to the finish. I think I win "mental toughness" points for sticking this one out!

* * *

After battling a brutally cold and snowy winter, I was ready to run the B & A Trail marathon. Training for this race had gone extraordinarily well, with just a few hiccups due to all the snow and ice storms. It was by far the toughest winter I had trained in, with record-breaking low temperatures on a regular basis, along with our fair share of snow and ice. I ran on a treadmill a few times, but eventually the treadmill started to hurt my foot so I had to steer clear of it. Coach Andrew continued to challenge me with new workouts, which kept things interesting.

Eleven days before the race, Greg broke his ankle while playing basketball. He hadn't played basketball in years (not since I'd known him) but his co-workers asked him to play, and so he did. He rolled his ankle going for the ball and it broke. I was naturally upset about this for obvious reasons, and it also meant that he wouldn't be able to run the marathon as planned. Despite his broken ankle, Greg still wanted to support me during this race by meeting me at various points on the course and handing me water bottles and gels.

It was unseasonably cold for late March. The temperature was 25 degrees at the beginning of the race, rising to about 32 by the end. Because I was accustomed to running in sub-freezing conditions all winter, the cold temperature didn't faze me one bit.

March 29, 2015

This morning I ran my 19th marathon: the B & A Trail Marathon in Maryland. I think there were only 300 runners and the whole thing took place on a paved trail. The race is well organized, with chip timing, mile-markers, aid stations, etc. But it definitely has no frills—no bands, no cheering squads, and nothing fancy.

My plan was to start the race at a pace of 8:20 for the first 6 miles and then gradually drop it down to 8:00 by the end. This would result in a finish time in the mid 3:30's. I mentally approached the first six miles as if I were doing a training run— nice and easy. The lack of fanfare made this easy to do—it was chill and relaxed. I decided to focus on my music and enjoy the experience. I purposely chose music that wasn't too hyped up.

In terms of fueling, my plan was to take a Honey Stinger gel every 40 minutes. I took my first one just after mile 5 and it went down well. I had experienced digestive issues during my last marathon in Columbus and I didn't want a repeat. I made sure to drink plenty of water with each gel.

Greg was waiting for me almost immediately after I finished my gel. He had brought our "game day" folding chair (which folds into something he can carry on his back) and was sitting along the side of the course. I ran past him and didn't say much, as I was in "the zone."

Mile 1: 8:21
Mile 2: 8:22
Mile 3: 8:27
Mile 4: 8:25
Mile 5: 8:14
Mile 6: 8:10

This race has a few inclines, but only one major hill. I knew to expect it during miles 7-8. It wasn't nearly as bad as I expected. It was kind of long, but not all that steep. I was thankful that I had run the Reston 10-miler four weeks ago, giving me confidence to run hills strongly. Those Reston hills were steeper than this one, and it was a whole race of hills! So this hill didn't even affect my pace.

I saw Greg just after mile 8, and I took a water bottle from him along with a Honey Stinger gel. I always run marathons with a hand-held water bottle so I don't have to stop at the water stations. The challenge with this morning's race was that I wasn't able to hold onto a bottle for very long before my hands would go completely numb. I wore big mittens with hand warmers inside of them (between my hand and the bottle) but they weren't enough to keep my hands from going numb. Thankfully I was able to toss bottles and keep getting new ones every time I saw Greg. Everything continued to feel good. The hill at mile 7 was a turnaround point, so miles 8-19 would be into the headwind. I was mentally prepared for it.

Mile 7: 8:03

Mile 8: 8:19
Mile 9: 8:18
Mile 10: 8:07
Mile 11: 7:56
Mile 12: 8:10

I knew I would see Greg at the halfway point or just before. I tossed my jacket to him, because I knew I would get warm wearing it even in below freezing temperatures. He gave me a new water bottle and Honey Stinger gel. I could feel my fingers going numb, so I kept my hands in fists around the hand warmers inside the mittens. I was still trying to carry the water bottle and the honey while doing this, which didn't work, and I dropped the honey. I decided not to pick it up because I had a spare tucked in my elastic waistband for an occasion just like this.

I crossed the halfway point in 1:48:30, which was in line with my plan. I was pleased with how everything was going, but I wasn't thinking too much about it. I was focused on running and making sure I got the water and fuel I needed. And that's pretty much it. I had my music, and I just needed to run in a straight line. This course has very few turns, no distractions, and it's easy to just "go" on autopilot. I started running mainly by feel at this point. I was no longer worried about going out too fast and I had executed exactly as planned.

I knew that the other turnaround was at mile 19 and I was counting down the miles to get there. This entire section was into a 10-12 mph sustained headwind and it was making my hands numb. It was a manageable amount of wind, although not particularly pleasant. But marathons aren't supposed to be pleasant!

I saw Greg at mile 17 and grabbed a water bottle and Honey Stinger gel. Holding that cold water bottle with my practically numb hand was nearly impossible, and it was definitely uncomfortable. I wanted to take my honey/water combo earlier than planned so I could toss the bottle. But I was very disciplined. I wanted to avoid digestive issues at all costs by not consuming too much sugar at once.

Mile 13: 8:10
Mile 14: 8:19

Mile 15: 8:05
Mile 16: 8:03
Mile 17: 8:08
Mile 18: 8:01
Mile 19: 7:59

After the turnaround point, things improved significantly. The wind was now at my back, I was done with my water bottle, and mentally I was running toward the finish instead of away from it. I was pretty sure that a PR was in the bag, but I didn't want to think too much about it. Instead, I focused on pushing hard and getting to the finish line without slowing down.

Mile 24 was incredibly challenging. The course veered off of the B & A trail onto a side bike path. Not only was this a detour in the opposite direction of the finish line, but I once again found myself running directly into a strong headwind—much stronger than before. It had to be at least 15-20 mph sustained. And . . . it was uphill. There's no sugar coating it—it sucked. Dealing with so much wind so late in the race and running in the opposite direction of the finish line seemed like a cruel joke. Despite all of this, I remained neutral. I made observations, but I didn't feel frustrated or angry. I just kept listening to Fall Out Boy through my headphones, telling me to hold on:

> I don't want to remember it all,
> The promises I made if you just hold on.
> Hold oooooon,
> Hold oooooon,
> Hold oooooon,
> Hold on.

I finally made it through mile 24 and found myself back on the B & A trail, ready to hammer it home. Things were tough. My legs hurt. I was tired, but I needed to keep the effort level high. It would have been so easy to slow down to an 8:30 pace and still PR. But I didn't want to do that—I wanted to continue to push to my max.

When I saw the mile-26 marker, I turned off my music so I could hear the volunteers' directions on where to go. That last 0.2 was directly into a headwind, but I was so motivated to get there that I just tore right through it.

Mile 20: 7:52
Mile 21: 8:04
Mile 22: 8:11
Mile 23: 8:18
Mile 24: 8:27
Mile 25: 8:07
Mile 26: 8:09
Last 0.31: (8:00 pace)

I crossed the finish line in 3:35:29. This is a PR by 4:31 and a Boston qualifying time by 4:31. Pure elation! I was finally able to run a race where all the pieces came together, and I made the most of it by focusing on the process: the pacing, nutrition, hydration, and mental resolve to stay positive. I ran the second half faster than the first half by over a minute, which demonstrates strong execution.

A big part of my approach was to get "in the zone" and stay there. I wasn't particularly happy or excited as I ran—I was simply focused and emotion-neutral. Even when the race threw curve balls like icy patches, a windy detour off the trail, and dropping my Honey Stinger gel, I didn't have an emotional reaction. I didn't feel happy, sad, frustrated, angry, excited, or anything like that. I was on autopilot and I didn't let anything bother me. I kept the finish line in sight, but I mentally broke the race into manageable chunks.

And now, I'm elated! I'm thoroughly enjoying my "later fun" because I truly earned it. I am looking forward to recovering and taking a week off of running. I might not even run a fall marathon and just wait until Boston 2016. I probably would not have gotten in with my 3:40:00 from Columbus, and now I am confident that I will.

In some ways, I feel like I got "the monkey off my back" by qualifying for Boston. But when I truly look at my journey, I realize that the monkey was gone long before this race—it had to have been in order for me to be so relaxed. Running a race like this is something that I have thought myself physically capable of for the past five years, but now I know I am also mentally capable of it.

CHAPTER 18:
BOSTON UNBOUND

November 28, 2015

My running is now reminiscent of 10 years ago, when I first started racing. It's easy for beginning runners to improve. Usually runners see major gains during the first several years, but then the law of diminishing returns kicks into effect, making PRs less frequent and smaller in size. This is particularly true for racing at shorter distances, where shaving just a few seconds off of one's time becomes challenging.

I think that many runners love the constant "high" they feel during their first 3-4 years of running, and then are forever in pursuit of that feeling again. It's similar to weight loss in anorexia, or even drug and gambling addictions. Runner's high is officially defined as the release of chemicals that make you feel good after about 30 minutes of running. But I also see it as the high of reaching new levels, testing boundaries and breaking through them.

This fall, I've set four significant PRs:
- 43:56 in the 10K (17 seconds)
- 1:37:33 in the half marathon (4 minutes, 7 seconds)
- 1:35:08 in the half marathon (2 minutes, 25 seconds)
- 20:51 in the 5K (38 seconds)

After years and years of training hard but not setting PRs (or small ones at best), I've finally pushed past both physical and mental barriers. Even though I am thrilled with these race results, the real achievement lies within *how* I was able to let go and let myself simply run.

* * *

"Everything happens for a reason," I said to Greg shortly after the B & A Trail Marathon, as we celebrated over beers. "The reason I struggled so much with the BQ was to make me a stronger person. If I had qualified early on, I wouldn't have learned everything I did."

"What if it happened to you so that you'd have a story?" asked Greg.

"That, too," I agreed. "It is quite the story."

"Why don't you write the story? You should turn all your blog posts into a book," he suggested.

I thought about Greg's idea for a while—months, in fact. As the Boston Marathon registration date drew closer, I realized that now was the time to write. Now, while everything was still fresh in my head and raw in my heart, was the time to tell my story.

* * *

My story ends with a beginning: everything I will take with me to Boston and through the rest of my life. There are eight key principles that have helped me overcome my mental barriers that I aim to adhere to in everything I do:

1. Separate yourself as a person from the things that you do.

Know who you are at your core, and how those core attributes enable you to do certain things. Core values and attributes like dedication, perseverance, compassion, honesty, and a slew of others define who you are. You bring them to whatever you do— your job, your relationships, and the pursuit of achievement.

At the beginning of my journey to Boston, I based my self worth on my accomplishments, and I wouldn't be happy with myself unless I was achieving my goals. My failure to qualify for Boston made me feel like I had failed as a person. This not only resulted in depression, but also the inability to relax and maximize my full physical potential during marathons. I am not a runner—I am a motivated, hard-working person who runs.

2. Focus on the things you can control, not on those that you can't.

While the achievement of a specific goal might not be within your complete control, the process is within your control. Focusing on things that you can't control results in anxiety and fear. You can't control what other people think or do, but you can control what you think and do. The irony of control is that the more you understand what you can and cannot control, the more in control you feel.

For the first 34 years of my life I felt as if anything I truly wanted was not in my control: my grades, the college I attended, my relationship status, my job, and even my running. I had very little tolerance for feeling out of control, and whenever something didn't go my way I would feel depressed or frustrated. My journey to Boston has taught me that even my own running isn't fully within my control, but I can feel more in control of it by focusing on the *process* rather than the outcome.

The process of racing is very simple. It involves preparation, nutrition, hydration, rest, and a pacing strategy that I can adjust if needed. Focusing on these elements instead of the weather, the hills, the race organization, and the finish time makes me feel more in control, and diminishes my anxiety.

3. Don't speculate—set expectations on the process, not the outcome.

While having goals is an important part of success, speculating on whether or not you will reach them is counter-productive. Don't try to predict the outcome, or it could become a self-fulfilling prophecy. Instead, set expectations for yourself that you know you can meet. For example, you can't control if you get a promotion at work, so don't expect one. Instead, expect that you will work as hard as you can at your job and do whatever is needed to get to the next level. On the flip side, if you think your boss doesn't like you, and therefore you won't get a promotion, then don't let that become a self-fulfilling prophecy.

I used to speculate on how the weather would affect my races, which would result in increased anxiety. To some extent, it's important to know what the weather will be so you can prepare and adjust accordingly. But ultimately, speculating on what will happen is wasted energy and counterproductive. Now when I race, I expect that I will push as hard as I can without giving up mentally. I'm focused on running my best race possible and I set high expectations on how I will accomplish that.

4. Stay neutral, and don't let emotions prevent you from doing your best.

To achieve something, what you like and dislike is usually irrelevant. If you don't like your work environment, for example, you can still do well if you focus on simply doing your job. What you "don't like" may make things more challenging, and the best response is to adjust where needed, and not get hung up on the fact that you don't like something. There are plenty of things in life not to like, but focusing on them will only drag you down further. The key to unlocking your full potential is to remain neutral when you encounter things you don't like, ignoring them as best you can.

With marathons, there are plenty of additional challenges that arise on top of running 26.2 miles: heat, hills, humidity, head-winds, crowding on the course, icy patches, jarring music, and a slew of other obstacles that could potentially arise. The key is to adjust my pace or my path if needed, and then continue on. What I like and don't like is irrelevant when it comes to running my best possible marathon. When I first set out to qualify for Boston, I would do just the opposite of this. I would shine a huge spotlight on anything that I didn't like, which made it difficult to have a positive attitude.

5. Seek out positive emotions.

Feeling happy, satisfied, accomplished, and/or excited doesn't always come naturally. Sometimes you simply need to make the decision to feel good about yourself and the situation you find yourself in. Life is too short to not seek out opportunities to find fulfillment and happiness. If you're used to viewing things through a negative lens, then it won't be easy or automatic to change your perspective. But if you put a concerted effort toward how you perceive things, then the positive feelings will start to flow more easily.

With racing, there is always a "buffet" of things to feed on. Sometimes that buffet is larger than others, and sometimes certain things (like a PR) aren't available. But that doesn't mean that I can't take what *is* available and enjoy it. Even if a race doesn't go as planned and I end up disappointed with my result, I can still find positive things to focus on. If my only reason for running is to set PRs, then I am spending a huge amount of my time on something that may lead to unhappiness. I now run to be a stronger person overall. I run to put myself in challenging situations and make myself stronger by overcoming them (or at least learning how to deal with them).

6. Quickly move past setbacks, focus on forging ahead.

It's easy to stew in your own depression and misery, and you may feel overpowered by these negative emotions. The key to moving past them is realizing that the longer you're down, the harder it will be to get back up. In other words—you are only making things worse for yourself. If you made a huge mistake or failed at something, review it, learn from it, and then move past it. Do not over-analyze it again and again. Make a list of key takeaways that will help you in the future and realize that you've gotten everything you needed out of the setback. Realize that it takes time and patience to achieve great things.

Whenever a marathon went badly for me, the depression and darkness would linger for weeks. And when it was time to run the next marathon, memories of how horrible the failure felt would haunt me, creating more pressure to meet my goal. For the first four years, each failed BQ attempt piled on top of the one before it, creating an avalanche of anxiety that I could not battle. When I finally learned to "shrug it off," I found that my race anxiety diminished significantly. And with less anxiety, I experienced fewer failures, so the ball started to roll in the opposite direction.

7. Don't compare yourself to other people.

What other people do is irrelevant to realizing your full

potential. Even if you are competing for a promotion or competing in a sport, you can't control what other people do, so it's not worth your mental energy focusing on it. You also can't control what other people think of you—all you can do is be your best self. Every time you find yourself making comparisons, remind yourself that you aren't helping yourself—you are hurting yourself.

When so many of my friends were qualifying for Boston and my marathon time wasn't budging, I felt horrible. I didn't think it was fair that I trained just as hard as they did, but without getting the same result. This line of thinking was bringing me down and creating even more demons to battle. Not only did I need to prove to myself that I was fast enough for Boston, but I needed to prove it to everyone else. This raised my anxiety level substantially, prohibiting me from relaxing and running to the best of my physical ability.

8. Seek out challenges—don't always play it safe.

Pushing past limits means that you have to test the limits. You'll never realize your full potential if you don't seek out opportunities to challenge yourself in new ways. These types of challenges take you out of your comfort zone, and may not be directly related to what you are trying to achieve—they may simply serve to make you stronger overall. The willingness to take chances and risk failure instead of playing it safe is the only way that you will discover what you are capable of.

I don't really need most of these mental toughness skills when I run races in ideal weather on flat courses when I am in peak condition. They come into play when I am faced with new challenges. Running in the heat makes me stronger. Running hilly races makes me stronger. I used to always seek out flat courses and flat places to train because I knew they'd be easier than hills. But now I seek out more challenging places to train and I don't shy away from the heat. I'm also not afraid to bonk in a race. Of course, it wouldn't be my preference, but in order to determine what I'm truly capable of, I have to test the limits and get out of my comfort zone.

I don't think that these takeaways are particularly ground breaking—they're simply skills that require practice and patience to learn. The key is to view them as skills and to commit to practicing them as frequently as possible, particularly in times of struggle. Eventually, they will become automatic as your overall mindset shifts from focusing on your desired outcome to the process of attaining it. I'll bring this mindset with me to Boston, and to wherever else life takes me.

EPILOGUE

April 19, 2016

It finally happened. After setting my sights on Boston in March 2008, I finally ran the race, 8 years later, and 10 years after running my first marathon in 2006. The Boston Marathon was my 20th marathon finish.

Race morning arrived, and after a semi-sleepless but restful night (not sleeping, but lying completely relaxed and still), I got ready for the race. Greg and I met our friend Amber in the hotel lobby and we walked to Boston Common where the buses would bring us to the start line in Hopkinton. I felt relaxed. It didn't really feel real. As we approached the bus loading area, I heard the announcer directing people. Then it started to feel real—with an official announcer telling people where to go and when. I said goodbye to Greg, gave him a hug, and he told me to look for him just before mile 20.

Amber and I boarded a bus immediately without having to wait in line, and it departed shortly after. The bus driver said the ride would be about 35 minutes, but in actuality it was 50. During the bus ride, Amber and I chatted about our training, our running history, and our jobs. Our husbands know each other from high school, but the two of us had only ever met via Facebook and

Strava. So there was a lot to talk about. I felt surprisingly calm. It didn't at all feel like I was about to run the Boston Marathon.

We arrived in the village, which was basically a huge field with tents. There were loads of porta potties, but there were loads of people to go along with them! We waited in line for about 20 minutes and then found a spot to sit down and relax. The starting village vibe was really exciting. There were people sleeping (or who appeared to be sleeping) on the ground with pillows and blankets. Many people were on the grassy area outside of the tent, but I knew it was really important to keep cool beforehand, so we stayed in the shade of the tent. I looked around me and realized that these runners were some of the fastest marathoners in the world. I took a moment to appreciate the fact that I was there, in Hopkinton, about to run the Boston Marathon with thousands of others who had also put in the hard work to get there.

They called our wave and before heading to the start line, I soaked my two "cooling towels" and cooling wrist bands in water and ditched my cover-up jacket. The walk from the village to the start line was about 3/4 of a mile, but it was so exciting and fun. There were volunteers and Hopkinton residents along the way offering us sunscreen, and there were even people who had black markers to write our names on our arms. I felt like a total rock star with so many people there cheering and helping us get ready.

As I stood in my corral I used my two cooling towels to keep myself cool, but they only went so far. I mainly focused on my shoulders and neck, and occasionally my face. I had also poured a ton of water onto my head before departing the village, and by the time I arrived at the start, it was already dry. At the start line, people were remarking how warm it was. Once person checked her phone and reported that it was 71 degrees. With no shade and not a single cloud in the sky, we were all baking before we even got started.

With five minutes to go, things started to feel more real—but part of me still didn't really feel like this was Boston. It was actually more surreal than anything. And I was really relaxed. The former me would have been really upset about how warm it was at the start line, but instead I thought to myself that we were are all in this together, and I was still going to run the best race I possibly could, no matter what the result.

Miles 1-4: Hopkinton and Ashland

The race started and I stayed relaxed. I was happy and confident and I knew exactly what I needed to do. The race was really crowded during these miles, as expected, and I didn't want to expend energy weaving through people, so I pretty much just went with the flow and kept everything feeling nice and easy. I found myself running slightly slower than an 8:00/mile pace, which seemed appropriate. My training runs and the Shamrock Half Marathon that I had run four weeks ago in 1:33:36 indicated that I had the fitness level to run a pace of 7:40, or perhaps even faster. But all of those runs were in temperatures that were 55 degrees or cooler, so I wasn't sure how much to adjust for the heat and sunshine. Knowing my history of running in similar conditions, I thought that 20 seconds/mile slower would be phenomenal, and 30 seconds/mile slower would still be pretty good. I decided to go for my "phenomenal" scenario, given that I had several cooling strategies.

I tossed one of my cooling towels at the start, but I kept the other one tucked into my skirt for the first few miles, and every few minutes I would use it to cool my face and neck. I also had cooling wrist bands that were made of the same material, and supposedly if you can keep your inner wrists cool, then your overall body temperature will be cooler. I also decided to dump 3-4 cups of water on myself at each water station—on my chest, over my head, and on the cooling wrist bands.

We reached the first water station at mile two. I carried a water bottle for drinking, and I only used the water station cups for tossing on myself. My plan was to drink water every 15 minutes, and take Salt Stick tabs every 45 minutes, as indicated on the bottle. I was careful not to drink too much. The water stations were really chaotic. Usually I avoid water stations in races by carrying my own bottle, but with this race, I took 3-4 cups at each station and doused myself with them.

My focus during these early miles was staying relaxed, keeping things feeling easy, going with the flow, and staying as cool as possible. I really didn't know how to best "save" my quads other than to prevent any start/stop motion and not to expend extra energy trying to defy the gravitational pull of the downhill. I tried to be really light on my feet and keep my entire body loose.

Mile 1: 8:11 (-111 ft)
Mile 2: 8:03 (-55 ft)
Mile 3: 8:01 (-50 ft)
Mile 4: 7:54 (-63 ft)

Miles 5-8: Framingham

The crowd was still thick at this point, but I finally felt like I could move about more freely than before. I focused on executing my race plan, which was drinking water every 15 minutes, using the cooling towel that I now had stored in my sports bra, and staying relaxed. I felt really good during these miles and the pace still felt ridiculously easy. It did not feel like marathon pace at all. It felt like I was out for an easy training run. So I wasn't worried that I was going out too fast.

The spectators were incredible. Usually I don't like a ton of people screaming and yelling as I run—I prefer peace and quiet so I can be in "zen" mode. But in the case of Boston, it was all about the fanfare and I was taking it all in. Even though I was really focused on executing my race strategy, I didn't want to forget that I was running the Boston Marathon, so I kept reminding myself to soak it all in and relish the experience. Usually when I run I am not focused on what goes on around me—I am more focused on execution. But in Boston, I didn't want to "miss" the experience! I also paid attention to the people running around me. Every single one of these people had qualified for Boston. They all knew what they were doing, at least to some extent!

Somewhere around mile 8, I saw a kid on the side of the course handing out bags of ice. YES! I took a bag from him, and put all of the ice directly into my sports bra, ditching the cooling towel. I knew this would cause major chafing, but I didn't care. I had heard that ice in the sports bra was a great way to stay cool, and so I did it. The ice jiggled around as I ran, and I hoped it would have the desired effect of cooling my core. It was still quite warm, with not a cloud in the sky. And the course was not shaded.

Mile 5: 8:04 (+8 ft)
Mile 6: 7:49 (-15 ft)
Mile 7: 7:54 (-12 ft)
Mile 8: 8:07 (-1 ft)

Miles 9-12: Natick

During mile 9, someone handed me an entire bottle of water. This was a lifesaver because I didn't have enough water in my handheld bottle to take my Generation UCAN gel with as planned. Without that extra bottle, I would have had to refill my own bottle at a water station, which would have cost me at least 20 seconds. So I was double-fisting it for about two miles. One water bottle in each hand was not comfortable, but it was better than having to stop to re-fill my own bottle.

Whenever I crossed over a timing mat, I got excited because I knew that Greg and others tracking me would see the split. I was feeling really strong as I crossed the 15K point, and my spirits were high. The spectators continued to line the streets with signs and cold towels, and I focused on soaking it all in. I also focused on keeping myself nice and soaked with 3-4 cups of water at each station. It was amazing how fast I would dry off between the water stations, only a mile apart! The sun was still high in the sky without a cloud in sight. I was expecting it to get cooler as we ran toward Boston, but I wasn't feeling that yet. These were the fastest miles of my race:

Mile 9: 7:58 (-12 ft)
Mile 10: 7:59 (+13 ft)
Mile 11: 8:12 (+28 ft)
Mile 12: 7:57 (-51 ft)

Miles 13-16: Wellesley

I could hear the Wellesley College women screaming well before I even arrived. The cheering at this point was insane! I can't even imagine screaming that loudly for so long. It was exhilarating and I felt amazing! I ditched my handheld water bottle at this point, and would rely on water stations for drinking.

I came through the halfway point in 1:45:39, which is an average pace of 8:03. I was primed to run a 3:31 at that point and I felt confident that I'd be able to do it. I had held my pace steady for the first half, according to plan, and my energy level still felt high. My quads started to feel sore at around mile 13, but I figured that was normal in Boston. They didn't feel "beat up" or "trashed," just noticeably sore, and I figured they would hold out for the rest of the race. Plus, I would use my glutes to power myself uphill and those felt great! Also, there wouldn't be a ton of downhill until the very end to cause my quads to hurt even more, so I thought I was in really great shape. As I approached mile marker 16, I knew that the tough stuff was about to start. I prepared myself mentally and reminded myself that this is what I had trained so hard for—this part.

Mile 13: 8:07 (0 ft)
Mile 14: 8:04 (-4 ft)
Mile 15: 8:11 (+23 ft)
Mile 16: 7:56 (-124 ft)

Miles 17-20: Newton

Greg McMillan had told me and his other athletes the day before that mile 17 was the mile to watch out for, and it's where most runners fall apart. He said that by that point, you've been running downhill for 16 miles, that even running on a flat surface feels like you need to expend more effort. He told us that we'd need to increase the effort level here to maintain the same pace. It should have felt relatively easy up until now, and now is when it would start feeling like a race. I told myself I would be strong during the first Newton hill at mile 17 and I wouldn't be one of those people who fell apart. I had run a smart race up until now. I felt good, and I would continue to execute my race strategy. I was still drinking water every 15 minutes, and I had taken two Salt Stick pills by the time I reached mile 20.

As I ran up the first hill, I reminded myself that this was 1 of 5 and that I would tackle them one a time, like how I tackle intervals on a track. There are actually only 4 Newton hills, but at the time I thought there were 5 for some reason. I slowed my pace slightly to get up the first hill, but I felt good and once I saw mile marker 17, I was so excited that I was still "in the game" and feeling good. It was then time for Newton hill #2. I pushed my way up it, telling myself to increase the effort level, and I made it to the top, no problem! Yes! Almost halfway done with the hills. Mile 19 was a nice treat because it was mainly downhill, and I felt pretty good going down it.

Okay, time for hill #3. This one was definitely harder than the others, but still manageable. I knew I just needed to make it through the hills and the rest of the race would be easier. I ran up the third hill slower than the first two, but still with a good deal of confidence. I could feel my quads, but the amount of pain felt sustainable. I was starting to feel tired and I was slowing down slightly, but I told myself it was just a rough patch and I would get over it.

I looked for Greg as I approached mile marker 20, but I didn't see him. I did, however, hear my friend Lynn screaming my name after I had almost passed her. I looked back and saw her and it was definitely a nice pick-me-up.

Mile 17: 8:26 (+74 ft)
Mile 18: 8:23 (+45 ft)
Mile 19: 8:16 (-32 ft)
Mile 20: 9:11 (+17 ft)

Mile 21: Heartbreak Hill

Before making my way up the hill, I gave myself a pep talk. I was feeling decent, considering it was mile 21, but things had definitely gotten hard. I told myself that I just needed to make it to the top and then the race would be mine.

This hill. THIS HILL . . . words cannot even describe the struggle. It was sheer torture trying to climb that thing. It felt like Mt. Everest even though I had run longer/steeper hills in training. I didn't look at my pace as I climbed. I focused on my form—using my glutes, leaning in, pumping my arms. There was a man nearby who looked to be in his 70's who was also trying to get up the hill. He said to me, "We'll make it to Boston one way or another!" I started to get ahead of him and I looked back and waved him toward me. "Come on!" I encouraged him. He ran with me for about 15 seconds and then fell behind me. "Come on!" I yelled back to him. It was helping me get up the hill by focusing on getting him up the hill. Ultimately, he couldn't keep up with my speedy 10:00 pace (note the sarcasm).

Major carnage everywhere. About half the field was walking. I told myself I would not walk. I would not walk up Heartbreak Hill, no matter what. When a hill gets hard for me, I usually look only about 15-20 feet ahead of me on the ground and I tell myself, "Just get to that point on the road." And then when I reach it, I pick another point ahead of me and I tell myself, "Just get to that point on the road." I do this until I am safely up the hill. It was truly a painful experience, and I am so glad I ran up the hill and passed a few people on it. Some people passed me, so I was worse off than some people, but better off than others.

I really was hoping that it would have cooled down by this point in the race, and maybe it had dropped a few degrees. If so, I couldn't feel it.

Mile 21: 10:06 (+96 ft)

Miles 22-24: Brighton and Brookline

There was a sign at the top of Heartbreak Hill that said "Top of Heartbreak Hill," and once I saw that sign I was so relieved. But I felt so dead once I reached the top, that I had come to the realization that the rest of the race would not be as rosy as I had originally anticipated.

Everything hurt. I was tired, my quads were worthless. Every step I took sent a pain through my quads and it was misery. Running hurt so much—even though mile 22 was downhill, I ran it at the same pace as Heartbreak Hill because I was just dead at that point. I couldn't muster any more energy.

There was also a bit of a headwind at this point. I welcomed it because it cooled me off, but it was contributing to the effort level I needed to expend to move forward. It was finally noticeably cooler, it was downhill, and yet I couldn't take advantage of these circumstances because I had baked during the first 22 miles.

I really didn't want to walk and I knew that walking would

only prolong the situation, but there were a few times during miles 23 and 24 when I had to stop for about 10 seconds at a time just to mentally reset. I came to the realization that I would not be re-qualifying for Boston again, and I was totally fine with that. I had no desire to revisit this punishing course again anytime soon (although I think I will be ready in 2018), so that was the least of my worries. I felt like death, so obviously *not* having an opportunity to come back next year and face this same challenge wasn't a concern!

It was the "survival shuffle" for these miles, and I was motivated by the fact that I wanted to really give 100% of myself to this race. I didn't want to look back on my experience thinking that I could have tried harder. So I tried as hard as I possibly could to make it through those final miles. I knew that there were loads of people tracking me and waiting for me to come through that 40K, and I wanted to get there as quickly as my body would allow me to.

Even though these miles are net downhill, there were still some nasty uphills thrown in there.

Mile 22: 10:04 (-80 ft)
Mile 23: 10:49 (-48 ft)
Mile 24: 10:31 (-50 ft)

Miles 25-26.4: Boston

I really, really wanted the race to be over, and I felt guilty for feeling that way. I was supposed to be having the time of my life! I had been dreaming about this for so long, and here I was, wanting it to be over. I told myself to feel joy, excitement, and pride! I told myself to savor the experience. But I hurt so badly. All I could focus on was the pain. I tried smiling. I constantly reminded myself that this was the Boston Marathon and couldn't I just really enjoy it? Nope, not happening. This was a death march all the way to the right turn on Hereford during the last mile.

I told myself that I really did not want to walk or stop. But there were some points where I did stop for a few seconds because the pain became unbearable. I was exhausted. My quads were on fire. Every step was torture. In order to prevent stopping and walking, I gave myself a new time goal—sub-3:50. I told myself that if I walked or stopped, I would be in the 3:50's and I really wouldn't be happy with that—mainly because it took me five years to break 3:50, so being in the 3:40's is like a whole different world to me.

When I made the right on Hereford, I used my time there to give myself a pep talk for Boylston. I told myself that I would run all the way down Boylston with everything I had in me. I would muster every ounce of energy I had to get there, and I would do it with a smile.

So down Boylston I ran. This was where the bombings happened. This was the most famed marathon finish line in the whole world. My spirits lifted. I truly felt like death, but I refused to let myself stop and I refused to focus on how awful I felt. Instead, I set my sights on the finish line arch, and went for it with all the passion I could find. I glanced down at my watch and I saw that a 3:48:xx was within my grasp, and I was determined to get it.

Mile 25: 9:41 (-41 ft)
Mile 26: 10:20 (+2 ft)
Final 0.4 9:29 (-2 ft)

The Finish and Beyond

I crossed the finish line and I was so happy to be done with the race! I wish I could say that this overwhelming sense of pride and achievement came over me, but the primary emotion was just relief. I was so glad that I didn't have to run one more step.

I knew that I only had to walk about 1/3 a mile to get to Greg in the family meeting area. I wanted to see him so badly. As I walked through the finish line shoot, I collected my medal and had my photo taken. The more I walked, the worse and worse I started to feel. I thought I would have felt better and better since I was recovering now, but that's not what happened. I almost made it to the family meeting area when I stopped walking and realized that I felt really, really bad. I felt weak. I felt dizzy and nauseous. And I was confused. Someone with a wheelchair approached me and I wanted them to wheel me to Greg, but they said they had to take me to the medical tent. So I had a choice—continue walking to

Greg (which is what I really wanted) or take a wheelchair ride to the medical tent. I broke down crying and started hyperventilating (mini panic attack) as I realized that the medical tent was my only option.

That medical tent was a well-oiled machine! They scanned my bib, checked me in and sent me to cot #12. They started asking me questions like what my name was and if I knew where I was, and my speech was far from normal. It was hard to get the words out. I spoke slowly and with slurred speech.

They laid me down on a cot and put my feet up. They asked me about my water consumption and I said I drank more water than I usually do, but I didn't think it was too much. Apparently I had the symptoms of hyponatremia, when your electrolytes become unbalanced due to lack of salt. I guess I sweated out a lot and didn't take enough Salt Stick pills with my water. The fact that I went to the bathroom so much before the race even started was probably an indication that I had perhaps drunk too much. It's really hard to get the right balance because I definitely did not want to become dehydrated. All of my training runs were in 55-degree weather or cooler, so this wasn't something I practiced recently.

They let me use a phone to call Greg and I told him I would meet him at the hotel, which was actually closer to the medical tent than the family meeting area. The medical tent people gave me a salty broth to drink and I felt much better after having that. Finally I was able to leave the medical tent and make my way to the hotel to meet Greg.

I was so happy to finally be re-united with him! I had so much to tell him and I didn't even know where to start. I was shivering, so the first order of business was to take a warm bath. After that, I really wanted to go to the McMillan post-race party, but I still felt sick, so I decided I just wanted to stay in the hotel room for the rest of the evening. I was bummed that I didn't get to enjoy any of the finish line festivities and celebratory events after all that hard work, but my body didn't want to move. I certainly didn't want to make myself look presentable to go outside, either!

My official finish time was 3:48:16. My Garmin clocked 26.4 miles at a pace of 8:38, with my marathon "effort" being a 3:46:36. I placed 13356 out of 26639 total runners. This puts me right in the middle of the field. However, the average finish time was 3:55:03, which means my time was about 7 minutes faster than average.

To further illustrate how rough these conditions were, only 36% of the field re-qualified for Boston 2017. This is the second-lowest re-qualifying rate in the past decade. The only race to surpass it was 2012, when temperatures rose into the 80's.

My bib number was 19448, which should mean my BQ time was the 19448th fastest, compared to my 13356 overall finish. So that was nice to see. Apparently almost everyone had a really tough day and missed their goals by 15-20 minutes—or even more. In 2015, when there was a sustained 20 mph headwind and rain, the average finish time was 3:46:28—about nine minutes faster! Plus, the field last year was not as competitive because the BQ cutoff time was smaller. So basically, the conditions this year sucked and most people struggled. That's all part of marathoning. You can't control the weather and you have to do the best you can with what you're given.

I'm extremely proud of myself for running through the end, keeping my mental state positive, and pushing through the pain. I've always struggled more than the average runner in the heat, and I've DNF'ed (did not finish) several marathons due to heat issues—when the weather wasn't as warm as Boston. This was a major lifetime milestone for me, and the experience seemed a bit surreal at times. I just couldn't believe I was running THE Boston Marathon. After eight long years.

As I said earlier, I will be ready to return to Boston in 2018. This experience was rich enough and painful enough to last a few years! Now that I know I can safely run 65+ miles a week, seven days a week, without getting burned out or injured, the sky's the limit. I do feel like I could have run a 3:25 if it were cooler yesterday, so I will chase that goal this fall and return to Boston in 2018.

If the weather had been cool, then I wouldn't have needed all of the mental toughness skills that I've learned over the years. The Boston Marathon was truly a test of mental endurance, and I passed with flying colors.

Elizabeth continues to blog at www.ElizabethClor.com.

Made in the USA
Middletown, DE
01 October 2016